F(r)ictionless Data

F(r)ictionless Data

Solutions for Better, Faster Decisions

Zane Hall

BUSINESS EXPERT PRESS

Leader in applied, concise business books

First published in 2025 by
Business Expert Press, LLC
222 East 46th Street, New York, NY 10017
www.businessexpertpress.com

ISBN-13: 978-1-63742-822-1 (hardcover)
ISBN-13: 978-1-63742-820-7 (paperback)
ISBN-13: 978-1-63742-821-4 (e-book)

Business Expert Press Big Data, Business Analytics, and
Smart Technology Collection

First edition: 2025

10 9 8 7 6 5 4 3 2 1

EU SAFETY REPRESENTATIVE
Mare Nostrum Group B.V.
Mauritskade 21D
1091 GC Amsterdam
The Netherlands
gpsr@mare-nostrum.co.uk

Dedicated to Tim Keller, who completely changed my view of faith and work, and thus changed my life.

DESCRIPTION

You've heard the promises of data: If you just unlock the hidden insights, you can win an unfair game. But for people at most companies, friction prevents data from flowing effortlessly into decisions. Technology alone won't make the connection for you. Neither will be finding more data; you've already got plenty. To *connect data with decisions*, you'll need to reverse the way data flows through all your systems and decisions.

If you're a business decision maker—a CEO, CIO, or CxO—you'll see the connection between a data strategy and the thousands of decisions people in your company make every day. If you're a data worker, you'll see how your work changes the direction of a company. And if you're an analyst—someone who bridges the gap between top-level decision makers and what's really happening in the business—you'll find a new vision of how to use data to transform your job and your company.

Instead of new technology offering tired promises to make your job easier, you'll find management solutions for better, faster decisions. **Unified data flows through your company, to everyone at the same time, improving business decisions through alignment and visibility, trust, and scale.**

That's Frictionless Decision Data.

CONTENTS

FOREWORD

Data is a strategic asset not a commodity or raw input. I learned this unique perspective from Zane through working with him for 20 years. As my career progressed from financial analyst to Chief Financial Officer (CFO), I initially viewed data only as an input—something to download to a spreadsheet, manipulate, analyze, draw conclusions from, and use to support decisions. I understood business applications—like SAP and Oracle—as tools to help automate my manual work. Again, data was just an input, and all the "value add" came from the business applications.

As I started to work with Zane, I noticed his focus on the data and not just the downstream business applications. By managing and organizing data strategically from the beginning, the workload of the financial analysts and the need for business applications (and their cost) were reduced dramatically. When I became a CFO, I greatly appreciated that Zane's approach resulted in a "single source of truth," critical for making decisions across any organization. Paradoxically, the end result of Zane's data management strategy is that everyone focuses on making the best business decisions and not on the data!

As executives and employees across the company began to understand the power of Zane's paradigm shift in data management, there became a strong desire to understand the "secret sauce" to make this happen. In his book, Zane reveals the ideas and framework to fully realize the benefits of his data management strategy. Every idea—like my personal favorite "exception reporting"—connects data to decisions in new, innovative ways.

Whether you work at a large, multibillion dollar company or a start-up, making good decisions is the obvious top priority, and it all starts with data. The quality of those decisions depends on the quality of your data management strategy.

Bruce Kiddoo
Technology CFO
Public company board director
Board member—San Onofre Parks Foundation
December 2024

PREFACE

Last year, sitting at the seafood restaurant on the San Clemente Pier with my long-time mentor, Bruce Kiddoo, I explained my crazy idea: I wanted to write a book on data strategies. This would be a huge time commitment and a huge risk; big decisions hinged on this, and it could all turn out to be a complete failure. Bruce wanted to know how committed I was to this idea, so he asked me very pointed questions, testing me on how much I believed in this project.

I told him about one of my favorite books, Malcom Gladwell's *The Tipping Point*. When Gladwell wrote the book over two decades ago, he described what it takes for an idea to go "viral"—a now-familiar term that describes how an idea catches on at scale. For an idea to really take off, it requires the talents of three types of people: "connectors," "salesmen," and "mavens." Mavens (according to Gladwell) are people who love an idea for the sake of the idea itself. Mavens not only collect information, but they also collect people to share that information with.

"You are absolutely a maven!" Bruce said. We both laughed. It was the perfect description of me and the perfect description of why I wanted to write this book. From my answers, it became clear:

Yes, I'm all-in on this idea.

I love to see people unified by a data foundation that everyone understands. I've seen this happen. I've seen it when a company works and thinks together, when people collaborate for the greater good, when they trust the data, and trust each other. It's a beautiful thing, and it brings out the maven joy in me.

I really do want to see organizations become transformed and advanced by good data strategy. Dorothy Sayers wrote that when you are motivated by the beauty of the work rather than simply your own personal career aspirations, then "the only reward the work can give you is the satisfaction of beholding its perfection. The work takes all and gives nothing but itself, and to serve the work is a labor of pure love."[1] Tim Keller said, "[I]f you do your work so well that by God's grace it helps others who can never thank you, or it helps those who come after you do it better, then you know you are 'serving the work' and truly loving your neighbor."[2]

That's my goal: If this book expands your perspective and unifies your company even in the smallest way, then I've succeeded.

INTRODUCTION

I just spent six months in a leaky boat,
Lucky just to keep afloat.
　　　　　　　　　—Split Enz, Time and Tide (album), 1982

My new Chief Information Officer (CIO) started the meeting by telling us that he had an urgent problem to discuss. Every C-level executive was complaining to him about data issues, all kinds of gaps, all summarized as a single problem:

The company lacked a business data strategy.

I found myself in this meeting after my small high-tech employer was acquired by a much larger company. I ended up, seemingly by accident, on the executive staff shortly after the deal closed. My new boss told the room, "Zane reports to me ... for now," communicating to me and everyone else that I could get demoted in a heartbeat.

It's a weird world, corporate America. Your stature in the organization often rests largely on what you say not what you do. Since I already have a problem talking too much, I decided I should be extra cautious in the first staff meeting. I kept quiet the whole time.

Most of my new colleagues didn't know this, but I'd spent the previous 20 years defining and driving data strategies at large tech firms. I had plenty to share on the topic, but with this crew, I had no street cred whatsoever. I told myself I'd only say something if asked—the less you say, the smarter you sound—so I listened patiently as multiple senior executives explained, at length, their opinions on what it takes to create a successful data strategy. As the meeting droned on, I guessed that the conversation might turn to me at some point, and I wondered if anything I could say would resonate. As the end of the meeting approached, the remarks forming in my mind grew more and more concise.

Sure enough, with three minutes left in the call, the CIO asked if I had anything to share. The room grew silent. At this point, I knew I had to pack 20 years of insight into a sentence or two, especially since the previous 57 minutes of longwinded opinions from the other executives didn't offer any fixes.

"Data is like water," I said. "If you don't manage it well, it will go everywhere and nowhere. You'll either drown in it or die of thirst."

The CIO jumped out of his chair. "Yes!!! It's exactly like that!" he yelled.

My word picture did the job. And then everyone looked back at me for more. At this point, the wisest thing I could have done was say nothing and left it at that. Instead, I thought, "Here's my chance!"

"…. But data is really like blood. It runs through every part of the company, keeping it alive. And this company is bleeding out," I added.

Then the video call ended, and everyone was in stunned silence. Time expired along with my credibility. That last word picture was just a little too vivid.

Later that day, I joked to my team that I had just ruined my new career at this company, and if I missed showing up for work one of these days, they would all know what happened. We all laughed. Nobody's job was in jeopardy. Working in data operations is more like being a plumber than a stock trader. If you don't have good pipes, you need more plumbers, not fewer. Even without a data strategy, it's still mission-critical for a company to keep the sewage from spilling out on the floor.

The IT team continued pursuing their main project, replacing the entire enterprise resource planning (ERP*) system. The best solution IT usually offers to solve a data problem is spending millions of dollars launching a multiyear "transformation" project. Spend as much money as you want on a new business system, but if it doesn't make decision data more accessible, you've wasted the money. Management just wants to improve business decisions—a simple goal—but how that works out amid a multiyear, multimillion dollar enterprise software project is hard to see. Decommissioning old systems always comes down to getting the data right.

Three weeks after that first staff meeting, one of my new colleagues was pitching the value of the new ERP project to the company's senior execs. Sure enough, at the end of the presentation, the CFO asked a simple question: "How will this project improve our decision making?"

After a long, pregnant pause, my colleague delivered his final slide. The answer? "Data is the lifeblood of a company." I felt vindicated and cheated all at the same time.

What's Your Data Strategy?

Truth is, when you are implementing a data strategy, you're taking responsibility for some of the biggest challenges facing a company. You're attempting to connect thousands of decisions together, across geographies, management levels, business units, functional groups, and so on. You're trying to unite people across a world of perspectives. You're trying to manage the thought of a corporate enterprise. It's a huge endeavor, and trying to limit scope doesn't make it easier.

---

* Enterprise resource planning systems, like SAP or Oracle.

What happens when it dawns on a corporate leader that they don't have a data strategy? When they realize that this is a far bigger problem than they'd ever considered, and they recognize that everyone around them has an opinion, but nobody has a solution? Do they default to spending money, or do they have the courage to actually change the way the entire organization thinks?

Most leaders in this situation think they need more technology. They don't; they need data strategy. But that's easier said than done. I'll show you how to build a business strategy with data and how to build it right. I'm not here to explain Business Intelligence (BI) to you; that ship sailed in the 2000s, when the data world was flat. Your data is not flat; it's all around you, and it touches every corner of your company. You need a completely new business data strategy to navigate the new data world.

Every time I meet a C-level executive, I ask them, "What's your data strategy?" Without fail, they always name technologies—as if parking your car in a different garage will make it drive faster—tacitly admitting they're still chasing a solution. They offer the same, tired, predictable answers: *"We're moving to the cloud," "we hired some data scientists," "we're using AI,"* or *"we got new analytics software!"* All good ideas, but none offering a management strategy.

To get value from your data, you need a management strategy not simply a technology.

The default management approach—spending money to fix problems—no longer works as businesses generate and compete on data more than ever before. Data drivenness must be understood in terms of business outcomes and management capabilities not the data you have stored. Landing an astronaut on the moon isn't simply a matter of possessing all the parts to build a rocket; the solution might look great on the launch pad, but it won't take you where you want to go.

I want to show you how to manage your data not what to buy. I want to show you a new kind of leader, a critical business partner who advances your profit instead of just keeping the lights on, the laptops running, and the cyber criminals at bay. I want to help you reach the goal of frictionless decision data.

Data is like water, and many have convinced you that a data lake will make you data-driven. But I am here to teach you how to value plumbing. You cannot live without water, but you also can drown in it. You can be flooded by it or die of thirst. You can have polluted water or fresh water. But nothing about your water happens by accident.

The Solution

Companies let their business data devolve into a state of nature. They buy into expensive technical solutions that are really just shortcuts, confirming that they don't know how to use data to manage their business. They expect data to improve their company's decisions, but instead they get unreliable data, people struggling to publish metrics, and disconnected decisions.

I have a solution: frictionless decision data.

Frictionless decision data (FDD) is unified data flowing through a company, to everyone at the same time, improving business decisions through alignment, visibility, trust, and scale. FDD is a framework, a strategy, and an end state.

The FDD framework: It's a design that creates *scale* by centralizing business logic and delivering data to the right people, at the right time, and with the right detail. The framework creates *trust* with processes that measure data quality, enforce accuracy, and link all the metrics together with master data.

The FDD strategy: It's a new way to manage data and decisions that software alone cannot deliver. It doesn't just try to make your situation a little better, it *reverses the direction* that data flows: Instead of flowing through people, frictionless data flows to people.

The FDD end state: It's an environment where data flows fast and free, where *visibility* and *alignment* make decisions agile and accurate, and secure and scaled. FDD helps your company make better decisions, and the way you manage and structure your data influences the way your company thinks

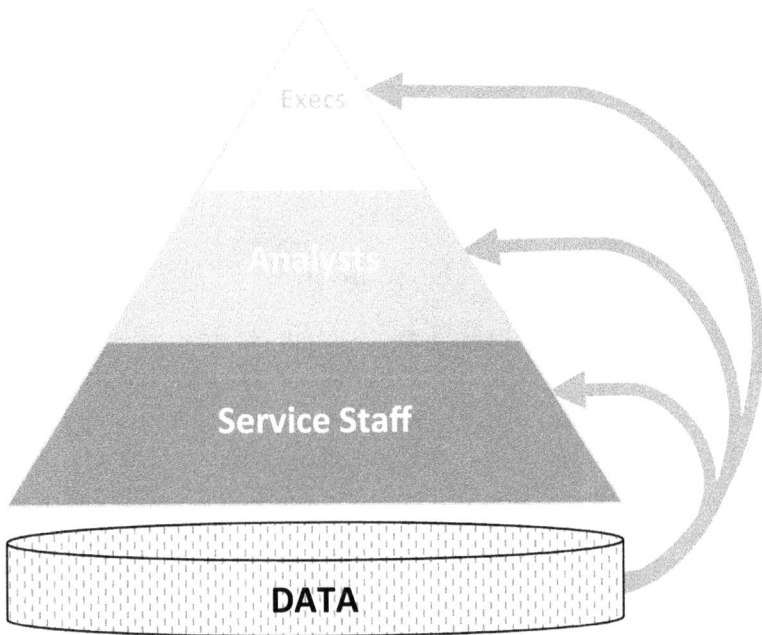

Figure I.1   Frictionless data flows directly to everyone at the same time

Visually, frictionless data flows through a company as shown in Figure 1.1. When business systems, business processes, and data flows align like this, decisions improve and accelerate.

I've written about both trust and scale in a way that anyone can understand. Whether you're an executive or a technical person, I'll help you broaden your awareness of what the business needs to make decisions at scale and an appreciation of what it takes to deliver it. I'll help people in both roles understand their own part in implementing a good data strategy.

I'll be right up front with you: This book is not going to give you a quick formula to become data-driven. Fixing a corporate data problem is more like recovering from an illness than repairing a car; there's no such thing as a shortcut. I want to give you and your company a new way of thinking, where data unifies decisions and people.

Managing corporate thought is an art. I want to teach you the art of the decision.

HOW TO READ THIS BOOK

Get out of the state, get out of the state you're in.
—B-52's, Your Own Private Idaho, 1978

Before I jump into what's coming, I'll make a few assumptions about you, the reader: You get it, and you're willing to take risks for the greater good. Data is critical for your company to stay competitive and for you to stay relevant.

You might be a top-level decision maker, a CFO, CIO, or Chief Data Officer (CDO). Maybe you're a hands-on data worker. A data engineer, architect, or report writer. Or you could be an analyst, someone in the middle, a financial, sales, or operations analyst, bridging the gap between the data and what the executives need to know.

If you're an executive decision maker, I'll give you an understanding of how technical decisions translate into the outcomes you're looking for. This book is not a technical manual, but implementing a data strategy changes the way people work, and I want to give you the understanding, conviction, and courage you need to make changes at your company.

If you're a hands-on practitioner, then I will help you understand the business context that makes your work so impactful. A good data architect makes or breaks the success of the strategy, so it's critical that you have the business vision required to connect the dots between technical decisions and expected outcomes.

And then, the analysts, everyone between the C-Suite, and the system engineer. You, the users of the data, are the real beneficiaries of this book. A data strategy is only successful if the analysts are successful. When you find value in the data, not just once in a while but every day, then real business impact happens. Business decisions start with you.

Defining Terms

A data strategy plays an outsized role in getting everyone in your company speaking the same language. Let's do the same here and align on some key terms. The rest of this book explains what FDD looks like; for now, let's contrast FDD with BI, Artificial Intelligence (AI), Machine Learning (ML), and Information Technology (IT).

Information Technology

First, **IT.** When we use this term in a corporate setting, it describes the people and processes that support the computer systems, software, data, and all the hardware required to provide these services.

The first business system teams I worked in were known as "Management Information Systems" or MIS departments. Today, it's much more common for companies to think of these teams as "IT."[†] The "management" strategy part diminished, and today IT people have about the same stature in the board room of a company as the cable guy coming to your home.

---

† A search of LinkedIn jobs shows that nationally, IT jobs outnumber MIS jobs by 38 percent, and by 75 percent in California.

IT teams typically divide into two parts: infrastructure and applications. Infrastructure jobs focus on what many refer to as "traditional IT": the network, servers, boundary security, and end-user hardware itself. Business applications jobs, on the other hand, focus on the software systems that business teams use to do their jobs. People working in these two disciplines—physical hardware and business process software—rarely cross over to the opposite side.

This changing focus of IT highlights a key contrast with FDD. FDD is first and foremost a business management strategy. Although it takes IT skills to manage the supporting hardware and software assets, the decision to adopt FDD will always be owned by business teams first.

Business Intelligence

You might have used **BI** systems before if you've spent time in a corporate setting. "BI" describes the set of strategies and technologies for analyzing business information and transforming it into outputs that support business decisions. Companies started creating BI teams about 20 years ago, and today, everyone accepts the idea that their business data is and should be a decision asset.

For me, the most important milestones in the BI world over the past 25 years were the tools analysts used on their computer desktops.

When I first encountered Microsoft Excel pivot tables in 1995, my world changed like it did for people watching color TV for the first time in the 1950s. Data suddenly became three-dimensional; analysts like me became explorers. After that, the tools (and the life of an analyst) stayed about the same until "data visualization" emerged in the 2010s. New visual tools like Tableau made heroes out of many analysts; data started flowing everywhere, more like a levee break than an irrigation system. Enterprise software vendors did a great job monetizing this trend by packaging BI solutions with business systems and selling specialized hardware to support it.

This story highlights the key difference between BI and FDD. BI focuses entirely on analytics, visualization, and data mining tools; it's a technology stack. FDD, in contrast with BI, is a management strategy not a technology. FDD considers the entire business data ecosystem of an organization, including the integration of data, processes, business systems, decision models, and people. While BI creates visibility for analysts, FDD gets trusted data flowing throughout your company.

Artificial Intelligence

Although awareness of **AI** ramped up dramatically since the launch of ChatGPT, **data science** and **ML** grew their footprint in business data management steadily since about 2013. Most business applications focus on improving data quality, making predictions, or upselling individual transactions (like recommending a product or a price).

Like BI, AI contrasts with FDD by its narrower focus. Better business decisions (hopefully) result from AI technology solutions, but aligning people and processes is a management capability not a technology. So, where does the line between an AI/ML strategy and FDD lie?

Few things are more important to an AI strategy than clean, reliable, trusted data. And isn't trust the main challenge with AI solutions today? The more strategic the decisions, the more human they become; people will only hand over decisions to automation when they feel they understand what they're letting go of. Trusted data starts at the foundation. Do this well and your AI/ML strategy will flourish.

Nicholas Carr stated this perfectly in his book *Superbloom*: "You can only get beyond the material [data] by going through the material, by suffering and surmounting its frictions. And that becomes harder and harder to accomplish or even to imagine the more that life is mediated by mechanisms of communication [AI]."

About Me

I've witnessed data transformations in many settings. Most of the ideas in this book emerged during my time at Broadcom Corporation and Maxim Integrated.

I started my career at a small semiconductor company[‡] in Orange County with a do-it-yourself data environment. As the Cost Accounting Manager, I taught myself database programming just so I could keep track of the inventory. That prepared me for the breakneck growth of Broadcom, where data moved at the speed of the internet.

Broadcom (and Wall Street) had so much confidence in their vision for the internet and wireless communications that they purposely overstaffed with overqualified people because they anticipated dramatic growth, seeing the internet business boom just around the corner. "Prepare the company to double in revenue every year" drove most hiring and planning decisions. We envisioned analytics as a key practice for a new kind of company and a new model for corporate thought. The vision was clear, but the details were not, so my team defined this practice through on-the-job training, and the company grew from start-up to an $8 billion a year enterprise over the first 10 years.

Launching a new ship in the right direction is a lot easier than turning around a giant ship midjourney. And creating a new business model (like Broadcom) is a lot easier than changing the direction of a company entrenched in its ways. That's the challenge that drew me to Maxim, an analog, 30-year-old Silicon Valley tech company. The business model was the same—semiconductors—but the data situation couldn't have been more different from Broadcom.

The strategies in this book quickly changed Maxim's data solutions from a severe pain point to a key planning and decision making platform. Leaders got real-time visibility into future demand and new product investments, shifting their focus toward the future instead of just trying to figure out yesterday's results.

Then Maxim got acquired by Analog Devices. The last thing I expected when this happened was that I'd get to lead the corporate data team to implement my data strategy. Not only was that experience

---

[‡] Silicon Systems, Inc., was purchased by TDK Semiconductor, which was purchased by Texas Instruments, then Maxim Integrated bought this business unit. The speed and frequency of corporate acquisitions in the semiconductor industry gave me a view into many operating models.

completely unexpected, but it also helped frame the picture I'd developed of how a data strategy transforms and unifies a company.

Through these experiences, I saw what a powerful impact a good data strategy has on business decisions in every setting. Then, my independent consulting work confirmed how easily these strategies translate to other industries. The most rational thing I could think of doing after that was to write a book about it—the book you're holding in your hands right now.

You might think the strategies I'm sharing in this book don't apply to you because they were all developed in the semiconductor industry. The opposite is true. These companies all used the same basic metrics, but almost every other factor affecting the success of their data strategy was different. By keeping the industry constant in these case studies, you'll clearly see the impact of all other variables.

Companies across most industries face common data challenges. An analytics director in health care explained to me his difficulties getting people to trust their data. An IT recruiter shared how most of his clients fill "shadow IT" roles with data workers. A university administrator described how the school's key management metrics use different logic every time they get prepared. Maybe revenue recognition is harder in a software company, maybe margins matter more when you're making widgets, and maybe fixed costs matter more when you're teaching students. But data quality and master data management are relevant in every case. Common data pain points affect almost every industry.

Navigating This Book

I'll share this new "FDD" approach with you in four parts:

- **See the friction**. The data isn't helping your company make decisions. I'll help you understand that frustration in detail, so you'll see what needs to change.
- **Reverse the flow**. Your data flows the wrong direction— that's the problem. Before we fix it, I'll help you see the "why" behind all the changes we'll make.

- **Build the framework**: To make this change, you need a deep understanding of the shape and flow of data. That's how we'll connect the dots between architecture and the way analysts think.
- **Influence the business**. Data should move in step with every business decision.

That means you'll need to change the way you do work. In this section, I'll show you specific management practices and policies that get your data trusted and free flowing.

With the book organized this way, you can take in the entire strategy cover to cover or jump to the part that's most relevant to your role. You'll find more detailed chapter introductions at the start of each section to help you navigate this book.

As you read through, you'll find many real-life examples you'll likely relate to. You'll find memorable anecdotes to remind you of core principles. You'll find counterintuitive ideas that help you see the big picture. But most importantly, I hope you discover a content-rich, game-changing approach to decision data that transforms the way your company manages its' business.

Yes, data is like water. Let's dive in.

PART 1

See the Friction

Companies everywhere feel the same frustration you might feel about your data: It's not helping your company make better decisions.

You'll need to understand that pain in more detail to appreciate just how much this friction hurts your company. Slow decisions, lack of collaborations, and fragile, unreliable data are just a few signs. Metrics depend on people instead of systems; just figuring out what happened in the past consumes everyone's time, leaving little focus on improving future results. You know you need to make a change.

But are you ready for that change? Your spirit might be willing, but you also need to consider the realities of your situation. A data strategy changes the way you manage, not just the technology you use.

Here's what you'll find in this section:

- **Friction.** A doctor gives a diagnosis because they understand the causes of the pain in more detail than the patient. To help find out where it really hurts, I'll offer seven signs of an ineffective data strategy to help locate the friction.
- **Change.** Changing course takes a lot more thought and effort than starting from scratch, but you'll find unique challenges in either case. In this chapter, I'll show you the experience of three different companies on their data strategy journey. By keeping the industry constant (semiconductors), you'll clearly see the variables that make or break your own success.
- **Alignment**. Real change happens from the inside out, and you'll face structural resistance. In this chapter, we'll take the idea of alignment down one level deeper and see the different types of gaps you need to close: process gaps, visibility gaps, and model gaps.

Any individual journey of transformation starts with a painful self-assessment. So too will your company's data strategy. You always need to face the facts before moving forward with a change. This dose of reality will help you start your data strategy journey with clear eyes and realistic expectations.

CHAPTER 1

FRICTION

I always knew that it would end this way,
That it's my destiny to be the King of Pain.
—The Police, Synchronicity (Album), 1986

Responding to questions about future consulting demand, Accenture CEO Julie Sweet said,

> The interest in gen AI has focused clients even more now on what we've been saying for a couple years ... you cannot use AI unless you have data. We just did a survey and 97 percent of executives think gen AI will transform their industry and company, but over half said data is the big challenge. So, we see a big opportunity to ... get their data **accessible**.[1]

The frustration expressed by these executives is not about a lack of data. It's the opposite: too much inaccessible data. But not just any data;

they're frustrated about their data. They're frustrated because their company generates tons of business data, but they can't rely on the information for many decisions. They're frustrated because they feel blind, not just about what's around the corner but even what's happening right now. They're frustrated because everybody has an opinion, but nobody has a real solution.

Everyone just marches on, overworking and overspending, always struggling to produce and publish the data and never experiencing its value.

Perhaps your company has yet to make the connection between these challenges and the need for a data strategy. Maybe your company recognizes the need for a data strategy but spends its money on software that can't keep its promise to solve the problem. Maybe your company has lots of data, but it's not data-driven, and your data stagnates, going underutilized in actual decision making.

Most decision makers think they are data-driven. They believe they are objective thinkers who consider the information in front of them and respond to it. And (they imagine) if everyone else would just take the same approach, we'd finally get something done. Data should unify people, we sense, but experience shows the opposite. Instead of adding clarity and bringing alignment, decisions become paralyzed. Indeed, more data has not made us more data-driven.

After 20 years of working with people all over the world, this story feels like Groundhog Day: It repeats in different places, functions, management levels, and industries.

The pain feels more like an infection than a broken bone. You know it's caused by neglect, but you still can't quite put your finger on the pain. How can a doctor know where to operate if you can't describe where it hurts?

Signs of an Ineffective Data Strategy

What does this lack of a data strategy look like? Here are seven signs that your company doesn't have a working solution.

Slow Decision Cycles

Instead of dynamic, fluid, daily, or weekly updates, decision cadences are built around lengthy reporting cycles that refresh monthly or even quarterly.

- Analysts and managers rack up overtime as they compile and interpret data before it gets presented to executives.
- New information takes weeks or months to get baked into projections.
- Teams waste time in meetings debating the accuracy and definitions of the metrics instead of plans to improve the results.

Limited Collaboration

Instead of working together, teams work in parallel to determine the numbers they need for their own business unit. Some indicators:

- Multiple systems process the same source data.
- Multiple definitions exist for the same metric, and depending on who you ask, you're likely to get a different number.
- Business teams publish data to anyone they want, resulting in too many reports with competing answers to similar questions. The graveyard for unused and unread reports grows and grows.

Fragile and Unreliable Data

Instead of a systematic, repeatable, hands-off flow, the path that data takes to get into an executive's view is mysterious, and the process to generate a metric might change every quarter. Some indicators:

- Executives can't trust the data they're given because it's gone through so many hands before it got to them.

- The number of stops the data makes along the way to an executive report is too complex. Mapped out visually, it looks like spaghetti.
- Few, if any, people know the path from aggregate metrics to the source data underneath it, leaving operations staff out of the loop when a detailed answer is needed.
- Because there are so many layered systems and so much layered logic, a new question about the data cannot be addressed immediately and often takes days, weeks, or months to answer.

Metrics Depend on People Instead of Systems

Instead of trusting the data and using it immediately for decisions, too many people audit the data at too many levels, and those people become part of the data machine. Some indicators:

- Data workers pile up unused vacation time because they (and everyone else) know that decision cycles stop when they're gone. If a key employee is not at work, a metric doesn't get published.
- Employees hunt for data instead of analyzing it. Finding and compiling data becomes the most valued business skill, and the person who masters this skill becomes a single point of failure for an entire department.
- Good analysts often leave for other jobs, looking for a place to use what they learned in school. The work experience isn't what they expected.

Low Business Visibility

Nobody uses the system to manage forecast data; so much energy gets spent on reporting what happened in the past, and there's no time for it. Business users assume they'll have to manage plan data on their own. Some indicators:

- Only top-level numbers exist for estimates of future results, if they exist in the reporting system at all. Most of your data looks backward.
- Key business teams get left out of the financial forecast process. Sales managers don't get much to say in sales forecasts, and product managers don't know the financial numbers they're measured against.
- The system doesn't keep track of previous forecasts, so people don't feel much sense of accountability. Analysts manage that data offline, and the system doesn't measure performance to plan anywhere except at the top level.
- What happens in the future is ... what happens.

High Spending

Like drug dealers, vendors tempt companies to spend more and more money to solve their problems. Instead of helping you build data into your decision processes, they make broad promises, guaranteeing new business insights and vastly improved decision agility, if only you embark on a multiyear, multimillion-dollar enterprise platform "transformation" project.

- Changing your entire data technology platform is constantly under discussion. Moving your system to the cloud is offered as a cure to business problems, as if solving climate change would fix your leaky faucet.
- Instead of delivering better data, new system implementations create decision making setbacks. It takes much longer than expected to recover.
- Many non-IT people carry titles that sound a lot like IT jobs. The business cannot wait for visibility, so they hire more staff to keep track of the data.

The Information Technology Team Adds Friction

Chief Information Officer (CIOs) want to be a business partner but are regarded only as a service organization. Some indicators:

- Few people believe that the IT department can contribute to real business decisions. The data remains static, not driving decisions but rather justifying them.
- The number of reports in the organization, if known, is very high, and so is the number of people involved in report writing. Empowering users sounds great until they realize they've lost control.
- IT reacts to data needs by creating more reports, and the ability to answer tomorrow's questions depends on IT resources.
- Every change requires tickets and approvals. Or worse, no tickets and no approvals. And seemingly simple improvements to reporting data take much longer than expected.

Working in the trenches managing corporate data, it's easy to lose sight of this simple truth: Data should help you and your company make better decisions. The first decision will be the hardest: the decision to change.

Yes, data is like water, but water can stagnate. Let's begin by understanding how much change you've got in front of you and how ready you are to pursue it.

CHAPTER 2

CHANGE

Where is the life that I recognize? Gone away.
But I won't cry for yesterday.
—Duran Duran, Ordinary World, 1993

At a critical point in my career, my mentor Bruce Kiddoo spoke truth to me.

Broadcom was easy—there was nothing to change. Maxim is a 30-year-old company, and our data is broken. If you want a real challenge, you need to find out if you can turn us around, not just jump on the right ship.

Maxim's data problems were handcuffing critical decisions, and they'd run out of solutions. They had installed a new forecast system but failed to dismantle the old one, making it even more difficult to use the data than before. Patchwork solutions failed to plug these visibility gaps; so much data was moving around—every day—that the reports just would not compile.

"All of our time is wasted finding and cleaning bad data," one senior director told me. "This is something I want to change, but at the moment it's next to impossible."

If you think you're ready to see your data strategy change, then you'll need to take stock of your circumstances to know where to start. Changing course normally follows failure, not success; it usually gets forced on you. When a situation reaches a crisis like this manager felt, it's a systematic problem. When a company collectively sees this, they're ready for a fresh start.

Are you and your company ready to step back and rethink how the data flows through your decisions?

Three Scenarios

Every company I've worked at started from a different place; one of them (or parts of all) probably represents your experience. To help you understand your own company's readiness for change, I'll compare these three semiconductor companies by common variables that predict change readiness. Each company represents an extreme end of the spectrum, which will help illustrate how much each factor impacts your strategy.

- Broadcom: a start-up that pioneered innovative data strategies from the earliest days of their company.
- Maxim Integrated: a 30-year-old tech company that recognized their data strategy wasn't working.
- Analog Devices: a technology giant with many competing data solutions and no central strategy.

I'll use some poetic license throughout this book to protect the privacy of the people I worked with and companies I've consulted at. Hopefully, this leads to clear, helpful messages. Analog Devices was my most recent employer, and both Broadcom and Maxim were since acquired.

Change Success Factors

Three common themes from these stories can help you assess your own situation: centralization, technical debt, and awareness of the gaps.

Centralization

Centralization includes not only the people and systems but more importantly the business logic that decision makers rely on. If the teams, systems, and business processes that manage data are spread out all over the organization, a lot more change will be needed.

Centralization doesn't mean you're stuck with one-size-fits-all solutions, but it does help create the leverage you expect from a data strategy. Some readers, especially the tech-inclined, will point to the wonders of a decentralized world where everyone handles everything on their own. I get it. I'll explain some of the downsides to that in the "Organization" chapter later.

Making a data strategy decision requires convincing people to get in line with the plan, and if that doesn't require anyone to give up ownership, the solutions can start right away.

Technical Debt

If you're not starting from scratch, you'll have some things to undo. That might be programs that move data, software that needs to be upgraded or replaced, or reports that people depend on even though they know they're wrong. IT people call this "technical debt," but plain English translations include "Byzantine," "needlessly intricate," or just "garbage."

Technical debt doesn't usually start with IT people. Poorly conceived data definitions usually create the most problems when IT writes code to work around them. Instead of classifying a customer status as "active" or "inactive," business teams come up with dozens of different values that only have meaning to the people who created them.

The longer the data goes unmanaged, the more data systems devolve to a state of nature. Business teams start depending on the very data pipelines and values you aim to get rid of. Visits to the dentist rarely end well if you only go when your teeth hurt.

When you're trying to change a company's data processes, remember that sophistication and simplicity usually go together. Managers prefer to ignore technical debt for the sake of short-term wins, so an honest assessment of this directly predicts the success of a new data strategy.

Awareness

Changing a data strategy requires changing the way people work, which doesn't happen organically. So, to turn things around, managers at all levels need to acknowledge the problems and agree to support change.

Your data might be out of control, but top management hasn't figured that out yet. Maybe that's because they've hired a huge staff to deal with it, and somehow, that seems okay. At the other end of the spectrum, your management may recognize the need to change without waiting for a data crisis. If that's you, you're off to a good start.

It doesn't matter how good or bad things are, you can move forward when the people at the top see the problem.

Starting From Scratch

In the 90s, companies didn't think they needed a data strategy. But as a start-up, Broadcom wasn't locked into old business models; innovation was the company's calling card, so management started a business data strategy before they even *had* any data. I don't think the leaders knew what that data strategy would look like—neither did I—but they understood that data-driven decisions would be an important part of their success.

The company's first product was a chip for high-speed modems, which essentially means Broadcom pioneered the broadband internet revolution of the 2000s. Wireless networks and Bluetooth connectivity solutions appeared on PowerPoint slides and Research and

Development (R&D) roadmaps long before consumers heard about them. The company was entirely focused not only on its own future but also the world's, predicting and planning for the historic changes in global communication.

An Integrated Mindset

This "integrated" perspective was built into the DNA of the company from the start because the company was made up almost entirely of circuit designers, top to bottom, with deep, end-to-end experience in the business.

Chip designers understand the concept of integration more than almost anyone; bringing together smaller components or combining functions into a single chip is the fundamental way chip companies compete. Engineering managers naturally expected instant response, perfect accuracy, and fully connected systems, all functioning as a single unit. That's integration: when all the parts of a system work together seamlessly in the most efficient way possible.

This same integrated approach is applied to business decision processes. Just like Broadcom's products, most business decisions focused on the future. And like a computer chip, the question about business processes was how to make every input work together with all the others (integration).

Companies with a lot of history tend to get distracted and spend all their analytic resources examining the data they already have—data about the past. Broadcom managers didn't have this problem, so they were able to focus on the integration of the business decision model itself. When it came to reporting data from the business systems, it was perfect when it lined up with the structure of the forecast data.

Here's a simple example of how this integration naturally happened. Broadcom had a product roadmap, reflecting its vision for where the market would go over the coming years and what products they would develop to serve that market. Keeping the roadmap current was an ongoing, organic exercise, owned by all the business units. A "return on investment" (ROI) analysis supported every product on the roadmap, and the data that made up that analysis lived* directly in the analytic system, with product managers constantly updating and versioning each product plan until it was approved.

Just about everyone was involved in forecasting the data. Revenue planning involved hundreds of business managers and salespeople, all projecting pricing and sales volumes for their products and customers as a part of their regular jobs. Thousands of engineers forecasted their project work directly in the analytics system. R&D work plans linked directly to the real-time sales projections. The finance team actively managed spending projections and rolled up integrated Profit and loss (P&L) forecasts in real time.

This flow created an immediate feedback loop. Planning processes (ROI plans) and business processes (selling, building, and shipping) were fully aligned. Practically, this created so much visibility and accountability that it virtually eliminated unprofitable "science projects" that people wanted to work on but didn't have any real market value.

Without a vision for integrated analytics, this green field scenario might lead to complete chaos. Centralized data management, a clear business model that everyone agreed on, and a strong management grasp of the data strategy made all the difference.

The company's success was unparalleled, growing to $8 billion revenue over the first 10 years.

Starting Over

Bruce was right. Maxim really was a chance to take a completely different approach to work and data. Instead of a means to an end

---

* Meaning it was "hosted" there. The underlying tables for planning applications were part of the data warehouse, segregated by schema. This allowed perfectly real-time reporting on the forecast, blended with historical data and plan versions. Allowing applications to write data into a data warehouse is generally seen by IT leaders as a violation of IT general control standards. This concern is valid when it comes to business transaction processing, but planning data is not a business transaction. Hosting data that exists only for BI purposes directly in the data warehouse is a specific FDD principle that will be discussed more in the "Architecture" chapter.

(career achievements), analytics became an opportunity for me to bring people and departments together. He might have oversold me because when I arrived at Maxim, people would say things like, "Oh, you're the guy Bruce said will fix our data." Yeah, give me a minute, okay?

Instantly, I was embroiled in weekly system and data outages. I spent my first three months trying to learn those systems and listening to complaints from users. The most senior guy on my team was moonlighting in a band, which I discovered because he was frequently snoring at his desk.

Finally, I asked a team of business leaders, "Do you want me to keep fixing these problems, or do you think we'd be better off abandoning the current platform and starting over?"

It took a lot of guts for the people in that room to give me the freedom to abandon the existing system. Maxim saw the value of a data strategy—IT already centrally managed the data—but the IT attempts to deliver it were a train wreck. Managers at all levels recognized it: Maxim was ready for a complete data strategy reset.

The technical debt was heavy. The company had three ERP systems and three forecasting systems. (How a company ends up in this situation is a story of its own.) In each case, IT installed a new system, but the legacy system never went away. The data systems made the problem worse, not better; daily data processing for metrics required 12 hours or more to complete—if it ever completed. All this complexity amounted to a massive amount of friction in the decision data.

This story plays out at companies all over corporate America: The company starts with a single system, adds another through acquisition, reorgs, or spinoffs, then decides that the best way to reduce the complexity of multiple systems is by adding yet another system. The truth is, subtraction by addition rarely works.

I call this situation "starting over." Maxim had big problems with the data, but they were mostly about the technical capabilities. Leadership already understood the value of a centrally managed approach, which is usually the hardest mountain to move.

Starting From Everywhere

When I started working at Analog Devices, I was excited to see what a data strategy looked like at a company much larger than any I had worked in before.

I didn't expect to find a company with a decentralized data strategy. There were about four dozen report development teams across the company, and the smallest data team was in IT. Instead of an enterprise strategy, departments mainly did their own reporting, sometimes competing for employees.

But Analog had just acquired Maxim, and that corporate merger created a new, urgent data problem: Nobody had a consolidated view of the business data. Management awareness suddenly appeared.

Surprisingly, I found myself in a role where this huge problem belonged to me, proving that if you come in with a vision, you end up with the responsibility to deliver it. I proposed a data strategy for the entire $12 billion enterprise. The worst that could happen was that I'd get rejected.

That didn't happen. About a year after the acquisition, my team launched a brand new data platform, using the frictionless decision data architecture to consolidate data for the whole enterprise. Technical debt remained throughout the business systems, but the new consolidated IT team recognized this, and the long road to alignment started.

Analog's data journey was not starting from scratch like Broadcom. It was not like Maxim, where the company recognized their need to reset. Instead, moving toward a data strategy for Analog was starting from everywhere. Centralizing the data strategy technically was a big accomplishment, but centralizing business logic was a much longer roadmap. The hard work of business alignment had just begun.

Change Agents

If you are starting from scratch (Broadcom), then the completeness of your vision matters most. Keeping the strategy pure and the implementation clean will extend your ability to see where decisions lead.

If you are starting over (Maxim), then your ability to get rid of old stuff—decommissioning old solutions—determines your success. And if you are starting from everywhere (Analog), you'll need to use influence first and foremost. You will become an evangelist for change at every level of the company. Getting top-level business support will determine how long your data strategy journey will take.

Don't jump in without a vision. Figure out what change scenario you're facing, and you'll then have a better idea where to start and what lies ahead.

Next, let's go one level deeper by understanding the decision gaps we'll need to close, what kind of resistance you'll encounter, and what data alignment looks like.

CHAPTER 3

ALIGNMENT

After Maxim IT teams worked over five years to automate their inventory valuation systems without completion, somehow, I ended up owning the project. It took my team another two years to get it done, mostly because the business rules were so complex, and the data quality was so poor. A semiconductor goes through hundreds of manufacturing steps, such as photolithography, etching, oxidation, metallization, packaging, and testing. Our costing algorithm applied 6 different rates to each step, which resulted in over 500 cost elements for every chip (which is smaller than your fingernail).

About a year and a half after we proudly launched the new system, the company decided to change its valuation rules to a much simpler method that just spread out ("allocated") the costs over all the steps evenly, like peanut butter. The business team was able to perform most of these calculations on a spreadsheet.

Getting trusted data flowing through a company depends on getting business processes and systems aligned. But (as I learned), it's even more important to get the people aligned on how they *think* about the business. It might help your company avoid throwing away seven years of work.

Three Dimensions, Not Two

In their seminal book, *Enterprise Architecture as Strategy*, Harvard professors Jeanne Ross, Peter Weill, and David Robertson propose an operating model they call "business modularity." Their thesis explains how optimizing your company architecture means aligning technology and business processes.[1] "Modularity" is a terrific description of this ideal state; it recognizes that when systems align with processes, people and technology *move together*.

Take the purchasing business process as an example. When you want to buy something, the first thing you do is place a request for approval. Your request routes to the approver, then to the purchasing department, who orders the product for you. The product arrives at your company location, where someone receives it and brings it to you. Then the vendor sends an invoice, which routes to you for approval and then gets paid. In business speak, that's called the *procure-to-pay* process.

The first thing I did when they asked me to manage this area at Maxim was compare all those steps with the systems that supported the process. I found that this process of buying a single item (like a computer mouse) went through 13 different software systems. From the business point of view, procuring my mouse was a single process, but the software systems were far more complex. IT spent a lot of time and money making that process look and feel like a single flow (Figure 3.1).

"Modularity" (as defined by the Harvard professors) means fully synchronizing the business process and the system process. This two-dimensional approach to business optimization made a lot of sense at that time (2006). But it did not account for the way business *decision*

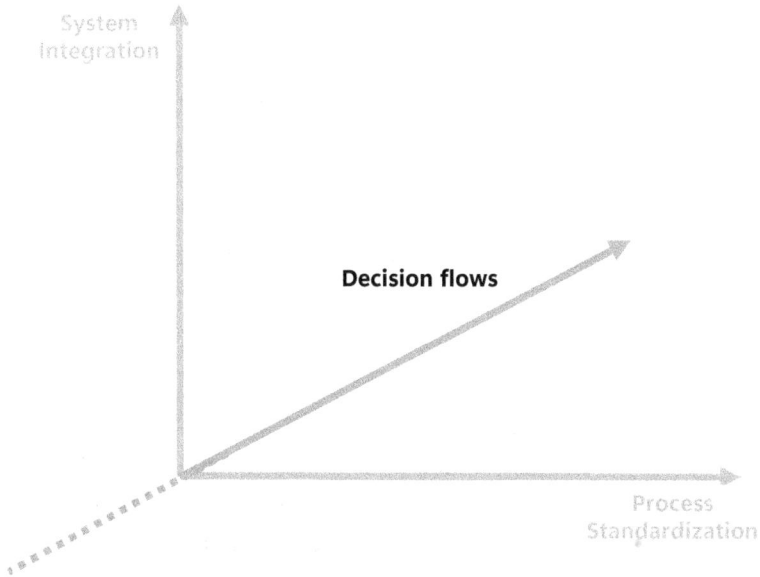

Figure 3.1 Frictionless data aligns not just business processes and systems but also decision flows

processes would accelerate and become much more important as a competitive advantage.

I'm proposing a three-dimensional model for business optimization: the alignment of systems, business processes, and *decision processes*. Aligning software systems with business processes makes your business more efficient; everything moves faster horizontally. But when both align with decision processes—when decision data becomes frictionless—everything moves faster vertically as well.

Decision Data Gaps

A company gets out of alignment when "decision data" gets disconnected from *financial* data. I call this disconnect **decision data gaps**. Financial statements show aggregated, high-level totals (like revenue) but don't contain any of the details (like customers or products) that inform business decisions. Yet the financial statements represent the best and only measure of "correct" data; your auditors signed off on it, and you've reported the numbers to Wall Street. Right or wrong, you'll need to match the numbers on the financial statements to know that you've captured all the data.

Decision data and financial data get disconnected in three directions:

- **Process gaps**. When the data in one system isn't aligning with data in another system, there's a process gap. Maybe your company is selling some services that you haven't set up in the order management system, so the teams must go outside the normal ordering process and perform manual billings.

  Postings to the financial system are another good example of this. If the numbers posted from the billing system don't align with the financial policies, then accountants plug these gaps manually with journal entries. The number of journal entries the accountants book every month gives you a good approximation of how many process gaps affect your systems.

- **Visibility gaps**. Business processes might be working just fine, but decision makers can't access the data in a form they understand. For example, system semantics often don't translate into the terms or categories decision makers use, so analysts spend most of their time translating the data. Analysts spend a lot of time plugging visibility gaps when your master data is not aligned across the company.

- **Model gaps**. When the forecasting models that your analysts use need different inputs than the reporting and business process systems support, you've got a model gap. For example, you might forecast sales at a "global" customer name. If there's no business process to group customers across geographies into a global customer name, you've got a model gap.

Three C-level executives at a publishing company described their data problem to me on different occasions. The company had spent a year replacing their business systems with new, industry standard

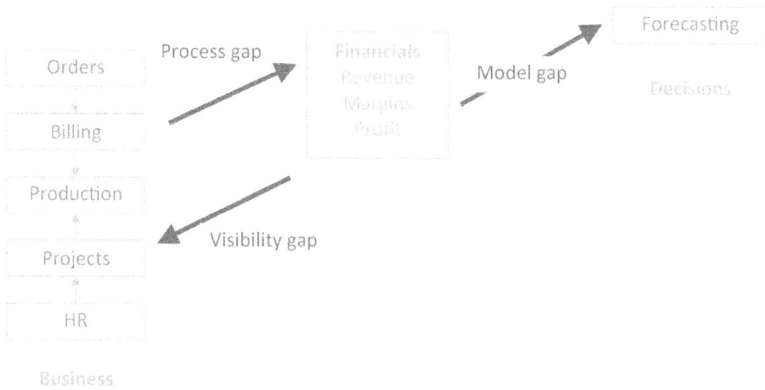

Figure 3.2 Financial data connects business activity to decisions, and gaps prevent companies from getting the most alignment from their data

applications, but the business data issues they'd set out to resolve didn't go away. The Chief Operating Officer (COO) described their financial processes as "fragile." The CIO explained them as "backward." The Chief Technology Officer (CTO) saw their situation as "change-resistant."

This company had breakdowns on all three levels. Core billing systems couldn't apply all the revenue recognition rules, so accountants plugged that gap with dozens of journal entries every month (process gap). They didn't have any reporting that accurately totaled their revenue, so analysts filled that gap with manual spreadsheets (visibility gap). And the manually prepared forecasts didn't balance with the actual results, adding friction to everyday decisions (thought model gap).

The good news for this company is that the gaps were not difficult to close. They didn't have significant technical debt—most of the systems were new. All levels of management were aware of the issue; whatever the issue was, it affected everyone.

But because they hadn't centralized their data strategy at any level, teams only understood their part of the problem. Figuring out the solution just took some teamwork to fix parts of all three areas—process integration, visibility, and metric definitions. That also resulted in agreements to centralize the business logic that linked the data together across all the dimensions (Figure 3.2).

A stubborn data problem might persist because of structural and organizational resistance, so take these head-on. Let's understand these next.

Structural Resistance

Michael Arena, in his excellent book *Adaptive Space*, makes the case that resistance to change permeates an organization.

"People feel like they hit a brick wall when they present their ideas and are stopped in their tracks by those who don't want the change or who see too many obstacles. And unfortunately," says Arena, "this doesn't come just from managers—it occurs at all levels within the organization."[2]

He's right, but this resistance isn't limited to the people or your organization's structure. Your *data structure* also creates resistance. If you want to make your company more agile, it's not just the big ideas that need a chance to be heard, it's also the thousands of daily decisions that suffer from data friction. Without a good data foundation supporting those decisions, changing your organization structure might not make any difference at all.

A funny example of how commonly companies get out of alignment like this happens in enterprise resource planning system implementations. SAP software is made in Germany, and the German acronym for "part number" is "FERT." There are other types of product names too, like "HALB" and "DIEN." Now most unindoctrinated people wouldn't have any idea what FERT or HALB mean, but everyone understands the term "part number." Yet people use these German acronyms all the time—they appear all over reporting and analytic systems. People end up translating these semantics constantly on their spreadsheets or in their minds, adding friction to everyday work for everyone.

Organizational Resistance

When Russian engineers tested the backup power systems at the Chernobyl nuclear plant in 1986, the systems didn't work as hoped.

Unwilling to acknowledge this, the crew didn't immediately restore the main power to stop the test, setting off a series of more mistakes that made the situation worse.

As explosions grew in severity, several employees went outside to get a clearer view of the damage. One survivor recounted that he looked up and saw a "very beautiful" beam of blue light (caused by ionized air glow) that appeared to be "flooding up into infinity."

Local officials weren't notified of the issue. People in nearby towns went about their regular business, but dozens of people fell ill with severe headaches, metallic tastes in their mouths, and uncontrollable fits of coughing and vomiting. The next morning, the Minister of Internal Affairs called the state government Chairwoman with his weekly update, and he added at the end of the call that there had been a fire at the nuclear plant, but it was put out, and everything was fine.

It wasn't until Swedish scientists detected radiation in the air that the Russian government defensively admitted something was wrong, a painful portrait of what can happen when information does not move up the management hierarchy easily.

Here's a real corporate example: The sales department issues two reports every week, one that shows the new sales for the week, and the second shows the lost sales for the week. The new sales report consistently reports larger numbers than the lost sales report, but the total sales for the company never actually grow. Eventually, something must give—investors won't ignore these contradicting trends forever. Finally, like the nuclear power plant, the data strategy melts down and gets reset.

When news travels *through people* and when managers hesitate to share negative information, things might blow up before they acknowledge problems.

Let's take alignment a step further: The way your data framework *aggregates* data plays an important part in management alignment. For example, when talking with a new client, I often ask two questions. "How many customers do you have?" and "Who is your top customer?" Rarely one person can answer both questions; the operations team knows they have 50,000 customers but doesn't know who the top customer is, while the executive knows exactly who the biggest customer is but will completely guess at the total customer count.

Friction, Change, Alignment. You want to move in this new direction. Hopefully I've convinced you of that. But changing your decision flow and the data that supports it isn't about making the situation a little better. To remove the friction, you'll need to make a complete turnaround. Next, I'll show you how to reverse the flow.

PART 2

Reverse the Flow

People experience friction with their data because of the way it moves. Or doesn't move, perhaps. The path it takes makes all the difference: friction results when data moves through *people*. To get rid of the friction, data must bypass the people; they're only adding to the confusion. You'll need to reverse the flow.

Getting people to let trusted data flow freely through company decisions depends on processes that keep data clean and accurate. But it's even more important to get the people aligned on how they *think* about the business. You're designing not only the data architecture but also the memories and expectations that the data represents. You're creating structures that help people think together about the past, present, and future of the business.

Here's what you'll find in this section:

Flow: In this chapter, we'll look at the decision flow of a company: how people think together, corporately. Look closely and you'll see how corporate decisions follow a sequence, a repeating, predictable flow. You'll either manage this flow or watch it devolve to a state of nature.

Personas: A good data strategy should help people in different roles get on the same page. So, you'll need to understand who they are and the types of questions they ask. Accessibility means something entirely different for executives, analysts, and service staff. Recognizing these differences helps you get the data flowing the right direction—and it helps you avoid one-size-fits-all solutions.

Trust: It's the most essential and yet most elusive goal of a data strategy. How do you build trust when people expect perfect accuracy and quality across hundreds of thousands of numbers, dimensions, and data points? People trust the data when they understand your process for both quality and accuracy. In this chapter, I'll explain a proven approach to deliver this kind of confidence.

Visibility: If you know you're measuring the right metrics, that's only half the battle; you also need to measure the metrics right. In this chapter, I'll show you how master data relationships and what-if analysis turn the entire landscape into insights about the future. Then we'll turn to the most practical matter yet, what makes a good dashboard.

Think of this section like that economics class you took that explained the entire monetary system. Rather than teaching you how to balance your checkbook (like your personal finance class might cover), it will help you make sense of all the hands-on work where you'll spend most of your time. I can't tell you what to do in every situation, but if you understand the "why" behind the "what," you'll be prepared to make solid decisions in any case.

CHAPTER 4

FLOW

Too much information running through my brain,
Too much information driving me insane.
                    —The Police, Ghost in the Machine, 1981

Cal Newport, the most counterintuitive business thinker writing today, threatens to upend everything in corporate America simply with the title of his book: *A World Without Email.*

A World Without Email argues that the scientific management approach applied by manufacturing companies a century ago also applies to knowledge work today. Back then, Frederick Winslow Taylor showed how companies could become more efficient by studying the work and experimenting with process changes. Today, Newport studies the way software development teams work, targeting their email communication with statements like "email reduces productivity," "email makes us miserable," and "email has a mind of its own," for example.

Newport states, "There's a belief, implicitly held by many knowledge workers, that the lack of processes in [knowledge work] is not just an unavoidable side effect of self-management but actually a smart way to work."[1] People enter the workplace, he says, preconditioned to see thought work as something that *should* be totally autonomous. He argues that communication in a company follows a workflow, and people should think together about their communication and find a more systematic approach.

How Decisions Flow

Newport's insight—that teams become more efficient when they understand project work as a workflow and collaborate this way—also helps us recognize how *data interacts* with corporate decisions. Look closely and you'll start to see how corporate decisions repeat and how they follow a sequence, a repeating, predictable flow. It's not just the way you communicate that needs to change. You need to change the way *business information* flows through your organization. You need a new way of interacting with data as an overall company.

Email adds chaos to communications, but unmanaged business data adds chaos to decisions. Cal Newport says it best:

> When you reduce [data] to a state of nature by allowing processes to unfold informally, the resulting behavior is anything but Utopian. Much as is observed in actual natural settings, in the informal process workplace, dominance hierarchies emerge … these setups are both demoralizing and staggeringly inefficient deployment of attention capital. But without a countervailing force, these hierarchies are often unavoidable.[2]

The idea that someone would tell you *how to think* comes paired with natural resistance from the individualistic, Western soul. It's almost the main attraction of data science today; perhaps you can find the needle in a haystack that's always been there but nobody else discovered. Your ticket to glory depends on the possibility that you might find a hidden knowledge nugget. Coordinated thinking just isn't the norm in our culture.

I want you, the data strategist, to understand the full significance of your role: You capture the histories and plans of a whole company. When decision makers think about what happened at their company in the past, where do they go? To the data. When they think about what will happen in the future, where do they go? To the data. If you just dump those memories into a lake, you're not just missing an opportunity, but you may also make the company's decisions much worse.

St. Augustine once said that the past is just a memory, and the future is only an expectation.* That's what you, the data strategist, have in your hands. Don't just let your company's decision workflows melt into an unmanaged mess; instead, give your data a mental health check and manage how the company thinks.

Henry Ford and Workflows

For about 20 years before Henry Ford changed the way cars were built, American car production was slow, unpredictable, and low volume. Frank and Charles Duryea of Springfield, Massachusetts, designed the first successful American gasoline automobile in 1893. By 1913, American companies made about 15,000 vehicles per year, and there were only about 300,000 cars in the United States. Did the people making cars even know it was a bad situation?

The way they made cars back then required specialized workers to go to each car and perform their craft, then go to the next car and do it again. In other words, the *people moved through* the car parts instead of car parts moving *to* the people. The car was finished when each worker independently completed their part of the work. By 1905, Frank Duryea's 50 workers were building 60 cars a year. Eventually, a fight among the company's owners led to the collapse of the business.

The way companies use business data today bears a striking resemblance to those car makers before 1913. We're about 20 years down the road into the big data world, and we haven't figured out how the

---

* See "Confessions," Book 10.

data should flow through decision processes. Just like those car builders before Henry Ford turned their process inside out, we're unaware that the data isn't flowing.

Henry Ford did not invent the car; he only applied the idea of assembly lines to building cars. Before the Model T, car building was an "asynchronous" workflow, a single process, but none of the steps happened in any particular order. Ford finally realized that the overall approach was backward. This required a lot more thought about the steps involved in building a car. Once they got the flow of work figured out, it was enormously powerful. By 1925, Ford was building about 10,000 Model Ts every day.

Ford's challenge was getting the right automobile parts to the right people at the right time, at the right level of finish. But for us, it's about delivering the right *information* to the right people at the right time, at the right level of finish.

IT people are great at capturing and moving data from place to place. I know, I'm one of them. We specialize in moving data from point A to point B. We copy data everywhere, even copies of copies. Superexpensive software solutions basically serve three functions: connect to data, copy it somewhere, and aggregate it. But instead of creating efficient information flows that accelerate thought, we create webs of data pipelines that challenge anyone to unravel them. Decision data workflows remain hierarchical and subjective, just like Cal Newport's description of corporate communications.

So, let's follow Newport's advice and take that intentional moment to think about how *companies* think. We've got piles of data and expensive technologies to manage it, but companies rarely form intentional thoughts about how to consume the data. Before we get to the frictionless decision data (FDD) architecture, we need to understand the structure of corporate thought.

Thought Architecture

In their 2008 classic bestseller, Nudge, Richard Thaler and Cass Sunstein argue that we are all "choice architects" at some level in our lives.[†] They call the framework of those choices the "heuristic lens," meaning the structure or environment in which teams think about the options. Technology is never neutral (they argue), and neither are your data management decisions (I argue). Your impact goes far beyond the code you deploy or the software you buy. They want us to recognize the impact of the way structured choices—good and bad—affect everyone's thinking.

Let's pause here for clarity on what I am *not* saying. When I talk about decision workflows, I'm describing the *structure* of the decision flow. I'm not trying to limit or control decisions themselves, quite the opposite. I'm trying to *remove friction* from decision making in your entire corporate enterprise. We recognize a structure—an architecture—in the way a company thinks about itself, its business, and its future. And that means that you, the data strategist, operate as a decision architect.

The starting "thought architecture" of a corporate enterprise typically remains unmanaged, just like Newport described communication frameworks. Analysts and managers constantly interpret data, adding their tweaks to the results, hiding or expanding details, and modifying the commentary, all before the data becomes visible to decision makers. Layers of management interpret the data at every level of review. This results in slow, fragile, and stale decision cycle times.

A frictionless data flow works the opposite way: It *depersonalizes* the message in the data, allowing decision makers freedom for more objectivity. Would you expect the message (the story the data tells) to get clearer when it flows through people? Will bad news easily flow up to the top of an organization? Maybe, but the phenomenon of bad news getting better as it gets communicated upward has an official name—the "Mum Effect"—given by the American Psychological

---

† Thaler and Sunstein recognized that their idea of choice architecture enters them into the debate between free will and determinism. They tried to reconcile this with their theory of "libertarian paternalism"—freedom of choice and control at the same time. My idea of the data strategist role as "removing friction" is a way to temper the enthusiasm of libertarian paternalism.

Association. When data travels *through* people, the incentives go the wrong direction because the message is linked to the person delivering it.

I'll take Thaler and Sunstein's point one step further: Analysts create thought structures every day without the help of IT. Examples of this include building spreadsheets, analyzing scenarios, and communicating conclusions to others.

When analysts model data on their own in isolation, each analyst has the chance to add value or add confusion to the decision flow. Your company's business systems create structure for transaction flows, but when it comes to decision flows, it's a spreadsheet-driven, free-for-all choice architecture. While it might seem like this diversity helps find insights, it costs an enormous amount of time for an analyst to manage their own models. Many who experience it describe it as the "wild west."

This "democratic" framework is not benign; it crowds out thought, eliminates repeatability, and potentially leads to disconnects. Friction results from the lack of a common analytic framework. But good management decisions flow better when we pay attention to the decision framework itself.

Data Flows

To find the default data flow in your company, try this experiment: Ask the Chief Financial Officer (CFO) how they receive data. I tried this with one CFO and found that he was compiling a key metric himself, using inputs (received by email) from about 10 different people. Nobody fully understood how those 10 people arrived at their inputs, but the company relied on the result for investor updates.

When numbers get delivered to your CFO, what happens between the original source and what's presented to them? Not simply the systems, but on whatever screen where they normally view the data. Follow the actual path of the numbers to her desktop, email, or conference room display.

Ask this question, and you may meet the most important person in your company.

That's been my experience over and over: There is always at least one person in the middle. You'll find someone who spends much of their day compiling data and delivering it to a senior executive. You'll find a preferred format. You'll find multiple data sources. And you'll find a set of business rules only known by the data deliverer. You might find an employee who hasn't taken a day off in years.

IT people call this person a "single point of failure." Sometimes companies justify this role by giving the person a real title, like "Data Steward." That employee may be defensive (wanting to hold onto the role), or they might be relieved that you (the data architect) have come to help. Sometimes the situation is much worse: A single "guru" provides data to entire departments, an informal risk, a single point of failure not just for analytics but also all your auditors, putting your entire financial compliance at risk.

Just adding more people to the data handling work might stabilize the situation a little, but it doesn't fundamentally change anything. In some ways (e.g., like in a nuclear plant meltdown), it makes the problem worse. The point of the FDD strategy is to get data flowing touch-free to all decision makers. That requires a whole different approach: changing the direction that the data flows.

Traditional Versus Frictionless Data Flows

Let's compare traditional decision flows to the data-driven decision flow.

In the traditional flow, data gets compiled—audited, summarized, modified, augmented, filtered, and enhanced—at every level, by many people and many departments. Analysts draw conclusions and steer the data toward their point of view. Layers of human and system interpretation get baked into every step along the way to the executive, leaving the message of the data softened and disconnected.

The FDD flow goes the opposite direction. Consensus, well-tested business logic gets applied consistently to all the data, the same way and at the same time. Analysts know the clear connections between what people see on the reports and what they see in the source systems. All reports, for all personae, use a single data source.

Change control governs the reporting logic in that source, meaning that people can't modify a business rule whenever they want; standard IT system controls ensure that new business logic gets tested and approved. Data owners know this and trust the report output more because the definitions can't change without being communicated first.

Data flows to every decision maker concurrently: The CEO receives data in their inbox at the same time the analysts get updates in their analytic tools. I want you to see the simple concept here: In the FDD solution, data *bypasses interpretation*. FDD doesn't try to make existing data flow more efficiently; instead, it makes data flow uphill and decisions flow downhill, without mediation.

Information travels up through your organization no matter what; the way it gets there is the whole point of this strategy. If you do not *reverse* the direction that data flows (to people instead of through people), you'll remain locked into a manual decision flow. Don't wait until you've spent millions of dollars and mountains of time installing a new solution before you realize this.

Reversing the Flow at Maxim

At Maxim, reversing the flow all came down to the email distribution list. We'd successfully automated the key sales metrics, satisfying the business definitions and analyst needs for every major team, but the executives still depended on a manual report emailed to them from a financial analyst. That analyst was ready to let the system deliver the metrics. Once the automated version was fully qualified, I sat down with the CFO for a conversation about the email.

Maybe you've noticed the irony here. I used Newport's critique of email to illustrate broken communication and decision flows, and now, my strategy all comes down to an email. But the point of this frictionless approach is not the *content* of the email—it's everyone's *awareness* of how the message flows. I'm using email to kill email (Figure 4.1).

"What I'm about to tell you might be hard to believe," I told him. "But if you let me put your name on this distribution list, all the

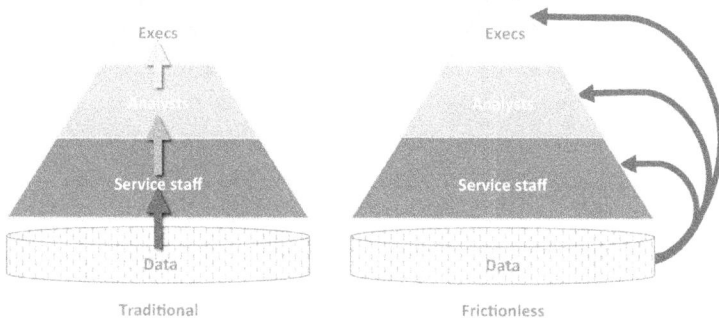

Figure 4.1 Traditional data flows pass through people to decision makers, while frictionless data flows to everyone at the same time

analysts will recognize that you are seeing the data at the same time as them. With your name in the 'To' field on this email, the entire flow of decisions at this company will reverse. Thought will accelerate."

And it did. Within a few weeks, the CEO asked to get on that distribution list. General managers started receiving their own versions filtered for their own business unit. Meetings changed across the company, and conversations between departments became more fluid. People started talking with each other about the business instead of debating about data.

Yes, in the end, it came down to changing an email to come from the system instead of the people, but it took all the work before that to get a consensus about the business logic and create the system to deliver it.

Data flows anywhere and everywhere that you allow it to flow. Now imagine your life if every time your family needed water, you had to go to a lake to get it. We all appreciate plumbing, but your kitchen faucet is not a good enough strategy for all your water needs. Delivering your data in the right amount, at the right time, at the right temperature, with confidence in its quality is your goal.

If traditional data flows go through people, who are those people? What will it take for them to take their hands off the faucet and allow data to flow freely to everyone? What does it look like when it all starts moving in the same direction? Let's understand these people—these "personas"—next.

CHAPTER 5

PERSONAS

I won't be fooled by a cheap cinematic trick.
It must have been just a cardboard cut-out of a man.
—Missing Persons, Walking In LA, 1982

A friend of mine works in Minneapolis as an MRI technician at a well-known hospital. Working the late shift one evening, a man in his mid-50s came in for an emergency scan. Now my friend makes everyone around her feel comfortable, calling everyone "brother" and "sister." But it wasn't so easy to get to know him since he came into the ER with a bodyguard. It wasn't until her kids explained to her, later that evening at home, that she had just gotten to know the lead singer of one of history's greatest rock bands.

My friend got to know the person, but she didn't know the "persona." I felt the same way about business systems when I started my career: They seemed like they were built for someone else.

Business software in the 1980s wasn't designed with the user in mind. Developers in this era often let a key stakeholder or designer create a solution mostly suited to their own personal tastes. They fell into a common trap that led to a lot of very strange business software solutions.

I experienced this firsthand at Texas Instruments, my first job. They called the accounting system "MODPLAN," which I guessed stood for "modern plan" but I'm not sure because there were no instructions or documentation. Everyone else—the people who'd worked there most of their lives—figured out how to use it long ago and knew all its idiosyncrasies. But the system designer didn't have somebody new like me in mind. Entering a journal entry in the system required putting a minus sign in front of the credits, and not knowing this led to some large-scale data entry mistakes that almost cost me my job.

In the 1990s, tech pioneer Alan Cooper proposed a new approach to software development: the "user experience movement." He defined software requirements for fictional characters who represented the typical person in a job function rather than one selected individual. These template users, which Cooper called "personas," helped standardize business processes and scale up software usage.* Just like X-ray technicians might tailor their treatments for rock stars differently than they would for pro athletes, software developers started using personas to help recognize the different needs of people in different job roles (like accountants and financial analysts).

I know, this all sounds obvious, trying to understand how people think and do work *before* building a system for them. But it wasn't obvious back then. Ironically, the software tools offered for data analysis today suffer from a similar problem: one-size-fits-all solutions.

But one-size-fits-all solutions (like just creating more dashboards) miss the simple truth: Not all data users interact with data the same way. They don't even ask the same kind of questions. Aligning a

---

* Of course, it helped vendors make a lot more money selling software! This advance also led to a new "glass cage" effect (see the Nicholas Carr book) where people just execute the work the system tells them to do without grasping why they're executing it. It sounds a little creepy when applied to decision flows because it looks like an attempt at thought control. But you can relax, we're not trying to do that here.

company means delivering the same data in different ways to different people. A data solution that makes this distinction will deliver the right data, to the right people, at the right time, at the right level of detail.

Types of FDD Personas

A good data strategy avoids a one-size-fits-all approach by distinguishing between the different ways different employees think. I'll map these usage scenarios to a set of template users, asking "how do people in roles like Joe and Sue normally interact with data?"

Three different personas use data for business decisions: executives, analysts, and service staff.[†] They ask different types of questions from a different point of view at a different rate. Some ask questions about business transactions; others ask questions about the future of the whole company. Some ask questions about the totals; others go directly to the details. Some ask the same question every day; others don't know their question until they see the data.

Accessibility means something entirely different for each of these people. Let's go through each category (Table 5.1).

Executives

Most people probably define an "executive" by their job title—a vice president, general manager, senior director, chief financial officer, or chief anything. Others might define them by the decisions they

Table 5.1 Data interactions by persona

Persona	Perspective	Frequency
Executive	Vertical/top down	Recurring
Analyst	Exploratory	Nonrecurring
Service staff	Horizontal/bottom up	Recurring

---

† (A fourth persona, "data workers," will be discussed in the chapter on architecture.)

make—decisions about the overall direction of a company, decisions about strategy rather than process. They spend most of their time managing the work rather than executing it.

I define executives by the way they interact with data. Executives usually care about tracking a predetermined set of metrics. They make directional decisions for the overall business or business unit, so they usually view data from the top down. In other words, they focus on *aggregates*. They ask questions like, "Are we measuring the right thing?" or "Is today's number what I expected?"

Executives usually start by looking at the result of the metric rather than the details, and they ask similar questions day after day; they know where they want the company to go, and they want to quickly verify if things are on track.

Service Staff

Service staff members maintain a business process. Think of a person who interacts with customers and handles the process and issues related to sales order processing. Think of a purchasing staff member who helps employees find and buy the supplies they need to do the work. Or think of an accountant entering journal entries.

Service staff care about business transactions: "Do I have the data that I need to execute my job, when I need it?" They use data records one at a time, a single business transaction that they move to the next step in the process. Their data questions focus on linear, horizontal processes. Data "friction" often slows down people like this who are just trying to do their job.

This was the case at Maxim. In my first week on the job, I asked (what seemed like) a simple question: Where can I find a list of all the products we sell? There wasn't a simple answer. Maxim was a multibillion dollar, global company; somehow, somewhere there must be a complete list of the products. High-volume product shipments churned through the transaction systems. Lots of parts appeared on the website. Part numbers showed up in a lot of places, but nobody really knew where they came from.

Then I discovered that the master list of parts for the entire company was managed by my own team in Microsoft Access. None of the other lists matched our list because every team added their own changes. These disconnects created daily friction for the service staff.

People on the service staff hate taking extra, unnecessary steps, like switching to another system to get data. They're not making analytic decisions; they only care about getting the right data onto the transaction. Data quality and availability matter most to them because real actions, like shipping a product or finding an item in the warehouse, depend on this. Service staff ask questions like, "Is the latest part version available? Is the customer zip code correct?" The rest of the organization depends on their work.

Ultimately my data team moved the entire company onto a single product master and customer master database in the enterprise systems. Simple reports of these centrally managed data sets got more use than any other report. You could almost hear the friction come to an end when this happened.

Analysts

Analysts specifically focus on gathering and interpreting data, drawing conclusions, and recommending actions to improve business results. They work in all parts of the business—sales, finance, operations, or marketing, with job titles like business analyst, financial analyst, (fill in the blank) analyst, or even manager. These people bridge the gap between questions from executives and the operational work. They're usually hands-on users of the data tools (like online queries, dashboards, downloads, and spreadsheets).

And they've got to be ready for anything. They don't know what data they need until someone asks them a question. And when it comes, they investigate and explore the data. What they find forms the story they'll read back to the exec, and they don't know how far the line of questioning will go.

It took my team about nine months to get Maxim's analytic framework setup and to put the tools into the hands of the analysts. They were in a tough predicament, tasked with answering questions but seriously limited by the tools available. To do their job well, analysts need a clear path—clear "lineage"—to navigate data from the aggregate numbers seen by the executive to the granular details managed by the service staff. Without this agility, Maxim's analysts felt demoralized in the same way that an automechanic might feel discouraged without a floor jack.

My team sat down with a room of 15 analysts in Maxim's corporate boardroom to demonstrate the first analytic solution from the new data platform. After an hour of pivoting, testing, and exploring the data, asking and answering many questions together, the meeting ended, and all the analysts gave my team high-fives on the way out. Believe me, this never happens to IT folks. But my data team had changed the everyday experience of an entire group of analysts. They became trusted partners that day.

One of those analysts spent 60 percent of his workweek compiling a key executive metric. He decided to directly partner with my data team, resulting in automation that freed him from this data prep time altogether. He shifted his time to business partnering and analysis, and he quickly rose through the corporate ranks to a vice president role (Figure 5.1).

Now, not everyone was happy. One analyst specifically told me that his job was to find, interpret, and deliver data to the CFO, and any attempt to circumvent that role wasn't welcome. It's easy for an analyst to get locked into the tactical part of their job and forget where they really can add value to a company. In either case, find the person doing the data prep, and you've found the focal point of the decision flow. Usually, they're an analyst who got stuck in the job.

Different personas, different questions, different data delivery methods through different tools, but the same, trusted data. It all comes from the same source, bypassing interpretation when the system delivers it directly to each persona. Helping different people work together with the same data links these personas together. Knowing the difference between these three personas helps you remove friction in the decision flows of your company.

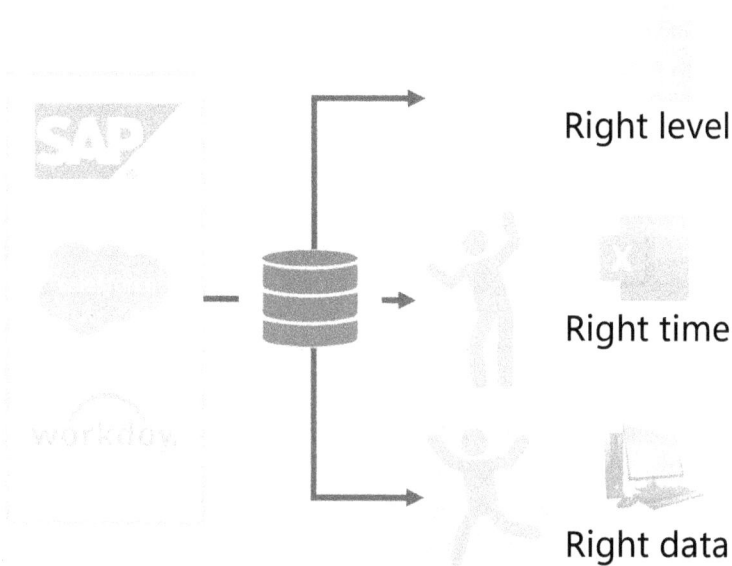

Figure 5.1 Frictionless decision data supports everyone with a single data solution while also supporting the different tools they use

This frictionless approach to data gets the same data flowing to different personas, helping them work with data in the way that fits them best. But getting them to let the data flow this way requires their trust. Next, I'll discuss the steps you can take to create trusted data.

CHAPTER 6

TRUST

I did not believe the information, just had to trust imagination.
—Peter Gabriel, Solisbury Hill, 1977

Philly sports fans care deeply about their teams, and they're notoriously known for both long suffering and loud impatience. The 2013–2016 Philadelphia 76ers were one of the worst performing teams in National Basketball Association (NBA) history. In the middle of that 2013 season, Sam Hinkie was hired as the team's new general manager when the previous GM didn't quite last a full year.

Hinkie introduced a new team management strategy known as "tanking." He decided (using analytics) that winning in the NBA was primarily a function of amassing top draft picks. So every time a player started to perform well, Hinkie would trade the player away to another team in exchange for more picks in the next draft. Everyone knew the plan; Hinkie was very public about it. But this forced fans to embrace the plan and be patient while enduring the losses of the team on the floor. It wasn't natural for Philly fans.

The team owner eventually lost his patience; however, and after three seasons, Hinkie was fired with a 19% win rate. Near the end of his tenure, ESPN interviewed one of the new young players, Tony Worten, who said, "They tell us every game, every day, 'Trust the process.' Just continue to build."

It wasn't long before fans were holding signs with this phrase. In fact, their 2014 top draft pick Joel Embiid got the nickname, "The Process" when he said in an interview, "I *am* the process." Sure enough, Hinkie's successors inherited today's championship caliber team.

I like this story not just because it's one of the most notorious "analytics" episodes of all time but also because it illustrates how trust is so essential and yet elusive. You can't buy trust; instead, you'll need to patiently work through the process of earning the trust of those you support. Your business teams will need to trust the process.

People trust data when they *understand* the process that keeps it clean and accurate.

Here's what I mean: You earn trust by following a process. In a large company, hundreds of thousands of numbers must be correct, all at the same time, all the time, in aggregate, and in detail, across all dimensions. One inaccurate data point, or even the perception of inaccuracy, will spoil the whole batch. Manually auditing data will never work; you'll need a systematic process to do it. A data team should present specific strategies—business processes—to help business teams keep their data clean and accurate.

Trust Part 1: Earning Trust Through Accuracy

When we're measuring accuracy, it starts with the money. Money makes the idea of accuracy very concrete; rather than an abstract concept, the conversations focus on dollars and cents. People pay you, you pay others, and both know what they spent and received. You report it to the government, and your auditors sign off on it.

One large company I advised had no clear process anywhere to compare their reporting data—which informed most management decisions—to the financial data. Knowing that at least the auditors would care about this, I kept asking questions, trying to locate where and at what level the comparisons to financial data happened.

I discovered that once every quarter, an IT programmer put together a spreadsheet for the outside auditors to explain how the analytic system numbers lined up with the external financial statements. I also discovered that this programmer dreaded working on the analysis every quarter, knowing how difficult it was to reconcile the numbers. Whether the CFO realized it or not, the company's financial integrity depended on his success in getting it right. It took him days to complete, yet he never got any recognition.

At some level, every company must reconcile its decision data to financial reports. It's not optional. Without a known process to "qualify" the numbers, there was no compelling reason for users to rely on the data published by the IT department. Most teams felt free to create their own reporting solutions. That's what happens when data teams don't create a process to keep data clean and accurate.

Integrated Equals Accurate

At Broadcom, management simply assumed that all the numbers were linked together as a single system. They expected that every number in a report related to every other figure presented to them.

For example, they expected that any number seen in a sales report would add up to match the revenue numbers everyone saw on Yahoo Financials. If they saw a number showing the annual cost per engineering staff member, they expected that you could multiply that rate by the total number of engineering staff, and it would match the R&D line on the income statement. Engineers didn't need to know how I would make this happen, but they certainly knew it was my job to make sure that the math worked.

When I started at Maxim Integrated, no such expectation existed. But once Maxim established a baseline of systematic, financially reconciled data, suddenly all the other business teams faced a choice: adopt the enterprise data or explain why they were not using the most accurate data set in the company.

The Process

What steps could you take right now to make this commitment at your company? First, make sure to include general ledger data in your data platform right from the start. Every report you create after that has a reference point.

Then, create a report for the single purpose of comparing other data sets to the financial totals; for example, compare the sales report to the general ledger totals for revenue. Show this reconciliation report to the Finance team and let them know it is a control they can count on. Email the report to them every month, so they know.

Finally, do whatever it takes to make sure the numbers match. That forces you to do a lot of research about why they don't match. That's the point. You'll close the gaps by adding more data to the data platform, by adding manual adjustments, or by fixing the business systems that send you data. But never stop chasing the systematic gaps and fixing them.

A systematic process like this "depersonalizes" accuracy; instead of people competing against each other for the "best" data, people and teams align to an external validation point that everyone can agree on. In this way, your process helps people trust not just the data but also each other.

This financial accuracy process helps build trust in these practical ways:

- **Recognizing issues sooner**. Following financial reconciliation processes means you'll validate overall accuracy at least 12 times a year. When reconciliations include some kind of automation, you start to recognize disconnects before they get out of control.
- **Reducing risk**. When business users rely on certain reports as part of their business processes (like pricing decisions), inaccurate data creates more risk than no data at all. A robust financial reconciliation process offsets this risk.
- **Forecasting**. People normally think about how much money they'll spend overall rather than how many checks

they'll write. Similarly, managers think about the future
at a higher level than everyday activity. The financial
framework creates a natural structure for this type of
forward-looking data. It helps you aggregate the very
detailed transaction data and align it with much less
detailed forecasts.

- **Building confidence**. Financial accuracy builds confidence
  that the overall numbers are correct, not just the details.
  The CFO, salesperson, and shipping clerk can all see
  accuracy from their own point of view. When people at
  every level use the same data set, it builds confidence.

Trust Part 2: Earning Trust Through Quality

Not all the data used by your company is numbers, so how do you
manage accuracy in all the other nonfinancial cases? You'll need a process to measure it.

W. Edward Deming was the OG* of data measurement, and the
grandfather of total quality management. He built his reputation in
Japan, right after World War II, when General MacArthur asked him
to help Japanese businesses get on their feet and restart the country's
economy. Deming combined a deep appreciation for the Japanese
people and their culture with a data-driven model; he measured everything and worked to continuously improve it.

Deming is reputed to have said, "In God we trust. All others must
bring data." His management philosophy went like this:

- *Always take a "system" perspective. If you're experiencing
  failures, 85 percent of the time it's systematic and not the
  employee's fault.*
- *Understand variation. Know what perfection looks like and
  measure it.*

---

* Original gangster.

Deming's principles form a great philosophical foundation for a frictionless decision data (FDD) strategy. You really can take a systematic approach to data quality, but it's not common to see a plan that actually works. Companies usually express a lot of passion (and frustration) about data quality, and that's about it.

For example, early in my career at Broadcom, the CEO stood up in front of all the employees at an all-hands meeting and said, "If you see something broken, fix it!" which inspired everyone and resonated with the overworking, overzealous high-tech spirit of the day; nobody was afraid of hard work.

I loved it too, but when it came to fixing data, his statement seemed a little haphazard. So, we decided to follow Deming's example and take a systematic approach. That's when this FDD data quality management (DQM) strategy was born.

Data Emergencies

A company without a plan for data quality will inevitably stumble into a data crisis at some point. Sure enough, about a year after I started at Maxim, we stumbled.

Dozens of purchase orders submitted by one employee kept coming directly to the CEO for approval. The requests were high volume and way below the value threshold normally required for CEO approval. Watching his growing inbox, the CEO concluded that the purchasing system was broken, picked up the phone, and colorfully expressed his dissatisfaction to the CFO and CIO.

Really, it was an HR problem. The purchasing system was working just fine, but the HR team missed a data error in the personnel system. The employee's boss had left the company, leaving her with a higher level of approval authority than her new boss. The system rules determined that the person with higher approval authority shouldn't require approval from people with lower limits, so approval requests systematically skipped up to the next highest approver—in this case, the CEO. The system was working as it should. It was just the data that was bad.

I'd been discussing my team's new, almost-ready data quality tool with the CFO before this crisis, so he found me and asked if I could create an "Exception Report." We discovered that 17 more people had the same data problem in the HR system, but they hadn't submitted any purchase requests yet.

The CEO was about to get flooded with still more approval requests, and the HR person responsible for maintaining this data was very grateful when the list showed up in her inbox, alerting her to all the data she needed to correct. Lesson learned: Never miss an opportunity to use a data crisis to your advantage.

Where do people most often notice bad data? My CEO first saw it in his inbox, but he didn't realize it was caused by bad data. When there's bad data in a report, everyone sees it, right there in their inbox or on their dashboard; good reports make bad data obvious. Managing data quality means *closing the loop* between what people see on reports and the source system where the error originated. Without this constant feedback loop, you're playing whack a mole.

The Process

Gaining trust in your data platform requires that you don't ignore bad data. But you also can't hide or mask bad data by writing code. You'll need a process.

So take this approach: Set up an exception reporting process *before* you build any metrics or analytics in your data platform. Bad data will destroy the best reports, and if you don't already have a plan for that, you'll be tempted to fix the issue the wrong way.

Train business teams to know what they should do when they see bad data—create an exception report. Find the person in the company who cares the most about quality data and let them know you're here to help. You'll give visibility to work that usually goes unrecognized.

Reactive Versus Proactive

Let's pause for a moment to consider two types of DQM approaches: reactive and proactive.

Reactive DQM means identifying bad data after it occurs and then fixing it (like the aforementioned HR example). Proactive DQM identifies the root cause—the business process or system gap—that allowed the bad data to exist and sets up the controls that ensure accurate data entry. Reactive DQM is a quick fix, while proactive DQM solves the issue for good.

Rarely will you find that every business transaction happens in a single system, regardless of company size; a single business process (like payments or order management) usually passes through multiple systems. The more complex your business architecture, the more data gaps you'll find. Therefore, you will always be working toward a proactive DQM end state, even while reactive DQM is your primary tool to get there.

Reversing the flow of data through decision processes depends on developing trust like I've described here. Letting you deliver the data to everyone at the same time requires people to let go of their manual reporting, "taking their hands off the wheel" so to speak. But it also depends on your ability to deliver that data at the right level of detail for everyone. I call that "visibility," and we'll explore that next.

CHAPTER 7

VISIBILITY

Look around, see what you do,
Everybody smiles at you.
> —Electric Light Orchestra, Mr. Blue, 1977

If you want to find the most comprehensive set of data known to Americans, look no further than Major League Baseball (MLB). There's no more extreme example of data "visibility." I tested this theory (that baseball produces the most widely known metrics) by asking Google, "What do Americans understand better, baseball data or weather data?" The result? "The effects of weather on baseball metrics."

The data on every pitch thrown in every game starts from about 1950. The age-old standard metric for pitching effectiveness, "earned run average," simply divides the number of runs given up (earned) by the number of innings a pitcher pitched. But the amount of information tracked about each pitch continues to grow over time, so much so that today, up to seven terabytes of data are gathered from each game.

When MLB started using video to measure pitching in 2015, Biola University student Jarvis Greiner (a film major on the school's baseball team) and Dr. Jason Wilson patented a new metric called "quality of pitch." The metric rates a pitch on how difficult it was to hit, regardless of who was in the batter's box. Instead of knowing just the speed and outcome (ball or strike, hit or miss) of a pitch, coaches and fans now get visibility into the rise, break point, knee distance, and total break distance, measured in inches or millimeters. With a metric like this, scouts can find a good pitcher even if he plays on a team with terrible defense or avoid a bad pitcher who looked good statistically only because he always faced awful batters. This amazing level of visibility means teams can predict a pitcher's success in the Major Leagues with a lot more confidence.

Unfortunately for the pitchers, visibility to hitting data also progressed at the same rate. In his classic 2003 book, *Moneyball*, Michael Lewis tells the story of how the small market Oakland A's used data to stay competitive with much wealthier teams who could afford big-name players. Fans and scouts alike had always thought the best batters were those who hit the most home runs. But the A's used data to discover that "on base percentage" better predicted wins for the team than home runs. They combined this insight with data on player salaries to field an inexpensive team that produced one of the longest winning streaks in baseball history.

This overwhelming amount of consistent, highly structured data illustrates the meaning of "visibility." Visibility describes how effectively a company measures a given metric. Good visibility means you can view the data from any perspective, at any level of detail, with any unit of measure, for the longest time horizon, past, present, and future.

Most companies and industries don't experience visibility like MLB, not just because they don't have as much data but also because they haven't developed as much consensus about how to measure their business. A friend of mine who leads the data practice at a large health insurance provider created something called the "Metrics That Matter report." He had to do this because the management team struggles to focus on the most common metric in their industry (engagement rate). He's created tons of visibility to the metric, but business alignment is their bigger challenge.

To achieve frictionless data, visibility alone is not enough. Frictionless data requires *both* business alignment and data visibility.

The semiconductor industry is much more like baseball in this respect; everyone in the business knows that "book-to-bill" ratio indicates their growth prospects. But not all semiconductor companies achieve baseball-like visibility. A company's level of visibility into their own data for the metric differentiates them from their competitors. I call this balance "metric effectiveness," illustrated in Figure 7.1.

Metric Effectiveness

A company with high visibility into the data but no business thought alignment is not frictionless. And when everyone in a company agrees

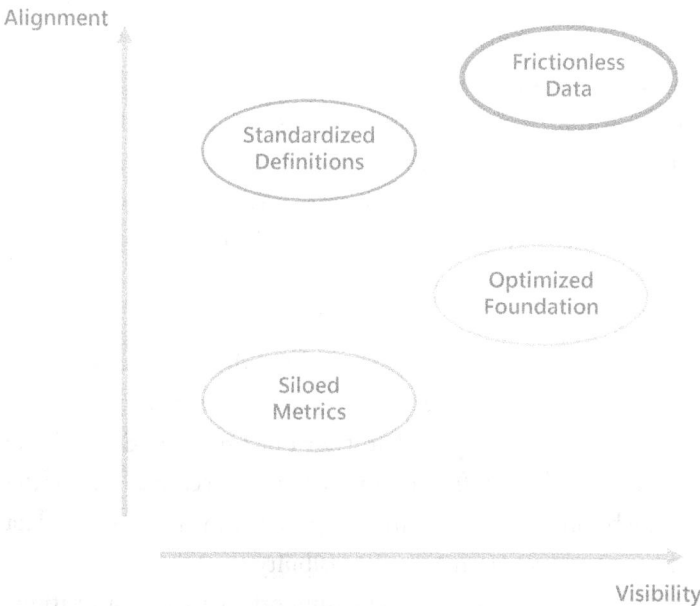

Figure 7.1 Frictionless metrics align the definitions people use and provide full visibility to the data

on what to measure, but the data solution can't deliver the visibility, they've also missed the mark. Measuring things right matters just as much as measuring the right things.

Focusing on visibility, three factors will impact where your company lands on this axis (Figure 7.1).

- **Core business process support.** When normal business processes naturally generate analytic data, it creates built-in visibility. For example, the Enterprise Resource Planning (ERP) systems should naturally update the open balance of an order when you ship some product. Companies without this capability struggle to recreate these relationships with reporting systems, an approach that limits detail and visibility.
- **Master data relationships.** When your company maintains clean master data for many dimensions, it creates visibility by helping you view business activity from more angles. Using my baseball example, if you know what college every player attended (not just their name and age), you might get visibility into what school to recruit from.
- **Indirect relationships.** Not all data sets relate to each other through natural business processes, such as linking sales opportunities to research and development projects. I call these "indirect data relationships." When the analytic system creates these links (with master data strategies), insights multiply exponentially.

That's what makes "big data" big: intersecting indirectly related data sets. The term "big data" emerged in the 1990s, referring to data that is so large, fast, or complex that it can't be understood with basic tools and strategies. This definition focuses on the technical side of the data, but the business process relationships that you create with a data strategy have much greater impact on visibility.

All these factors—business process support, master data relationships, and indirect relationships—depend on the master data structures in your data platform. An inadequate master data strategy will always limit business visibility. You'll hear a lot more about master data in this book; for now, I'll explain the value of master data along two dimensions: horizontal (linking business processes) and vertical (linking decision processes).

Horizontal Value

When I talk about the horizontal dimension of master data, I mean that it works across *linear, sequential business processes.* Business processes (like buying and selling) execute one transaction at a time, in a fixed sequence, from the beginning to the end. A product (master data) links all the activity together as the common thread across the business processes. I call this "*horizontal value.*"

For example, in supply chain business processes (known as procure to pay), you buy ingredients for a product, build the product, and then store it in the warehouse. The product ID links the processes together. Hamburger chains fill demand differently than computer hardware makers, but from a data management point of view, the same linearity applies.

Success in these horizontal business processes depends on consistent, identical master data across all the systems involved. "Integration"— the utopian ideal behind large-scale ERP implementations—means that everything happens as a single system, single process, and one collaborative unit. Everything becomes faster and simpler when all the master data is consistent throughout the process.

Vertical Value

Master data creates "vertical value" when it helps managers understand what's happening in the business, giving them visibility. Unlike business processes, business decisions usually depend on the master data groupings (hierarchies).

Management decisions require context. If sales were $50,000 in a day (total revenue) by filling 2,300 orders (total order count), decision makers don't know if that is good or bad unless they know what the total was yesterday, for example. They also won't learn much about what happened if you can only calculate the grand totals. They need data groupings that give visibility to "product line" data, the next level down from the grand total. They need to see the forest, not just the trees, but they also want to know *which part* of the forest they're looking at.

This concept of hierarchies isn't technical at all—you already use them every day. For example, the city you live in is part of a county, which is part of a state, part of a country, and part of a continent, and this hierarchy is a great way to make sense of the population of the United States. Making sense of data is mostly a matter of applying hierarchies to large amounts of data.* In other words, master data aligns decision workflows. That's *"vertical value"* (Figure 7.2).

Horizontal and vertical values create visibility through the structure of the data. But frictionless data isn't static; you want to improve decisions about the future, not just see what's happening now. Let's explore these forward-looking decisions next.

Future Visibility

When Marty McFly arrived in the year 1955 and Lorraine fell in love with him instead of George, he recognized that he had to change this result. Marty had a distinct advantage over Lorraine and George: He knew they were his future parents, and if they didn't become a family, Marty would cease to exist.

As this example from *Back to the Future* shows, when it comes to making decisions, information about the potential outcomes is the most important data. A good data strategy creates *continuity* between past and future data. Plan data is simply inputs from managers about future business, and building up the forecast through the analytic system shifts everyone's focus forward.

---

* There are far more ways to get value from data beyond summarization, something we'll cover in the modeling chapter. For now, we're limiting scope to master data.

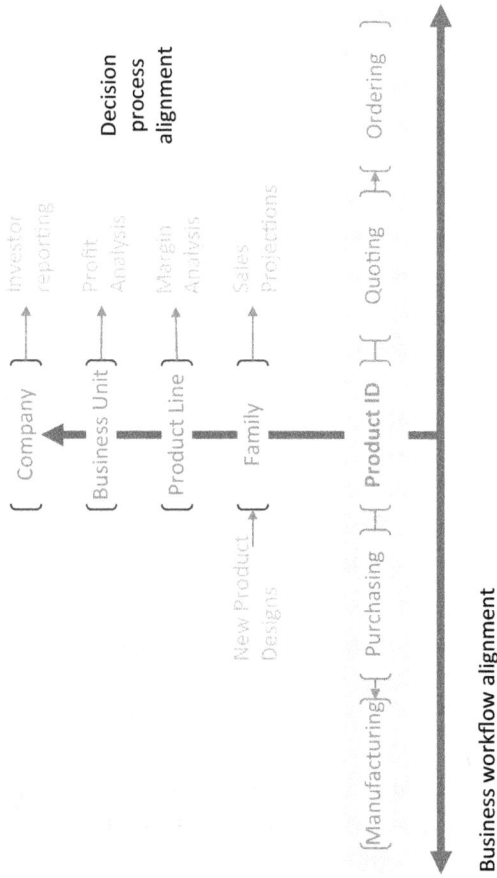

Business workflow alignment

Figure 7.2 *Master data creates visibility by linking horizontal business processes and vertical decision data*

But a good data strategy doesn't stop at gathering inputs about the future. "What-if analysis" (which I also call "scenario modeling") uses the analytic system itself to evaluate different options and see the impact on the overall data set. You can evaluate the *shape* of the overall business (structural scenarios) or the impact of individual variables on business decisions (input scenarios).

Here's an example of structural what-if analysis. Maxim realigned (shuffled) products and business units a lot. With structural scenario modeling, business managers worked with the data team to evaluate business unit margins under different business unit configurations. Because the master data relationships were managed in the analytic system directly, it was easy—taking less than a day—to change the product line relationships and view the new business unit totals with the normal reports.

Now an example of input scenario modeling. When Broadcom replaced their forecasting system and built planning capabilities directly into the data platform, they could change a single cost in the manufacturing materials (like the cost of silicon) and see the impact on the three-year P&L outlook. Instantly. Companies rarely experience real, integrated scenario modeling like this. It's also the ultimate promise of frictionless decision data (FDD).

In the next chapter, we will review strategies to manage plan data. For now, let's consider visibility in the most practical sense: the decision data that appears on an executive's desktop.

What Makes a Good Dashboard?

When Luke Skywalker saw the target on the X-wing fighter dashboard—something he'd visualized before—he knew his shot would have the expected outcome. Freedom in the galaxy was at hand. Everyone in the Rebellion forces knew the goal and understood their part in making it happen.[†]

---

† "Rogue One" reminded us that a lot of thought and effort went into defining the target Luke had in his sights.

But what about your own dashboard? Does it help your team clearly visualize the goals and inspire the actions needed to get there? Does it help everyone get on the same page?

First, consider the meaning of a dashboard. The common definition is a graphical user interface that provides at-a-glance views of data.

Even though the term originated with automobiles, people (and Google) today understand this term first and foremost as tool that presents data. That makes sense because just like driving a car, decision makers need to keep their eyes on the most important measure of what's happening right now. Without timely, accurate information, the driver might make a bad guess about the car's speed and hit a curve in the road going too fast.

Let's face it: For executives, the assessment of your data strategy all comes down to the dashboard, regardless of how well you've built the overall data solution. Everyone follows their lead; whatever data the CEO uses for decisions suddenly matters to everyone else in the company. Since a dashboard usually fits on one page, it follows that the better your dashboard, the easier it is to get everyone in the company on the same page, literally.

So, let's consider what makes a good dashboard. I suggest three key qualities. A good dashboard is newsy, actionable, and visual.

Newsy

If your dashboard isn't showing something new every day, then it is not guiding your daily decision making. If data on your dashboard only changes once a month, then it isn't a dashboard.

People make a common design mistake by showing a lot of history on their dashboard. But historical data doesn't—and shouldn't—change. A good dashboard should only show enough history to give context to today's decisions. Another common mistake is showing too much or too little granularity. A sales order dashboard might show every order taken yesterday (too much detail) or just the quarter total (too little detail). You must find the granularity balance that will drive both the executive summary and the operator's action.

Bottom line: Your dashboard should show something new every day, just like your favorite online newspaper.

Actionable

Always keep in mind the relationship between *operational changes* and *metric effects*. A good metric is actionable when people receiving the data have a clear understanding of what the dashboard measures and what it takes to improve it. IT people call this "lineage," the process of understanding how data flows from the source to the metric. A good metric always has this clear connection.

The key metric at my first job, Disneyland, was theme park attendance. My boss Tom had a little box on his desk with red LED numbers that constantly rolled over, like a slot machine. Whenever someone walked through a turnstile, the number increased. It seemed like pure magic.

It wasn't magic, it was good data lineage. Bad data lineage is a lot more common. At one company I advised, nobody knew how the finance department calculated the daily sales numbers. The IT guy who wrote that program left the company a decade earlier. I noticed once that when the Gregorian calendar changed, the metric also changed, and nobody could explain why. Finance relied on a number that everyone else in the company ignored.

Visual

Unlike plain numbers, visuals communicate value—red is bad, big is more, trending up is good. Always consider how you can combine these elements to tell a better story. Visualization delivers a much more effective message by combining color, size, and shape with numbers. The message usually gets clearer when you remove unnecessary data, lines, and labels. You don't have to be an artist to do this, just use visuals to put more information into less space.

Trust, Flow, Alignment, Visibility—that's what the FDD strategy delivers. If I've convinced you of this, then you understand the importance of these values. Next, let's understand the solution: the FDD foundation itself.

PART 3

Build the Framework

Like building a house from the ground up, building a good data framework requires many skills: understanding the foundation, the architecture, and how to manage it. In this section, I'll take you right down into the details of how the FDD system does this. Here's what you'll find:

Foundation: It starts by identifying different data types and managing them appropriately. If you don't make these distinctions, the data foundation won't support the rest of the architecture.

In this chapter, I'll use four key characteristics of data that help you recognize different data types: the source (where it comes from), velocity (how fast it changes), retention (what to keep), and volume (or amount of data). Then, I'll show you how to use this knowledge to get the most value from the data.

Architecture: When you start building the warehouse, you'll need to follow the structural design to know where to put the logic, how to store the data, and where to allow access. In this chapter, I'll explain the layers of the architecture and how each one helps you manage business logic and the flow of the data. We'll also connect the dots between the technical solution and the business outcomes you expect.

Organization: When your company starts using the system, centrally managing the strategy makes it grow and scale up. But centralization isn't a simple either-or decision; instead, I'll explain how to decide where and when centralization makes sense for your company. You'll need to keep the outcomes in mind the whole time, but you'll also need strategies to help the organization make the tough decisions.

Agility: No matter how much you plan, unexpected things will happen. You've got to be able to stay on your feet. In this chapter, I'll show you four "nimble practices" that will put you on a good footing when the inevitable changes come. Think of this chapter as stretching exercises before the big game.

There's a reason why I left these chapters for the second half of this book: if you didn't first understand the business purposes of the FDD strategy, you might not appreciate why it makes sense to invest this much time into building the system. You'll need that confidence to help you avoid shortcuts and jump straight to the metrics.

Seeing the friction and reversing the flow got you ready for this; now let's build the framework.

CHAPTER 8

FOUNDATION

You set my feet upon a rock,
Made my footsteps firm.

—U2, 40, 1983

Someone once said that a wise person builds their house on a rock, while the foolish person builds their house on sand.* The foundation—the ground beneath the house—determines what will happen when the rains come down, the streams rise, and the winds blow and beat against the house. The foolish person didn't expect their house to collapse—they only built it on a shifting foundation because they couldn't tell the difference between rocks and sand. They looked the same.

Maybe you're in the same situation with your data—you started building the house before preparing the foundation, and now things are getting a little shaky. So, let's do some excavation and understand what it takes to build a good data foundation.

---

* The New Testament Gospel of Matthew, 7:24.

A solid data foundation distinguishes between different data types. Different types of data behave differently, create business value differently, and require different management approaches.

Building on Water

"Building a house on sand" paints a clear picture of bad ideas. But in the data world, many people thought that building their foundation on water made a lot of sense. I'm not making this up.

I compared data solutions to a lake in the chapters "Water" and "Flow," but I'm not the first to use this analogy. This idea emerged around the late 2000s. The term "data lake" was popularized by James Dixon, the founder and chief technology officer of Pentaho, in a blog post he wrote in 2010. "The data lake is a large body of water in a more natural state. The contents of the data lake stream in from a source to fill the lake, and various users of the lake can come to examine, dive in, or take samples."

The concept behind the data lake was to create a centralized repository that could hold massive amounts of data, stored in its raw form. Advocates hoped that data scientists, analysts, and others would discover insights or some kind of value from this set of assorted raw data sources all saved in one place.[†]

This approach made sense to people because the common business analytics approach was the democratic model, where success meant enabling "citizen developers," and the most valued skill was "mining" data. It sounded so appealing: Everyone wanted to be a technologist, and IT teams didn't know anything about the business anyway (they assumed).

Ironically, the idea of citizen developers shut out IT departments from becoming business partners and using their data expertise as a business strategy. Instead, a new phenomenon emerged at about the same time: "shadow IT,"[‡] where functional teams hired their own data staff and created a disconnected mosaic of solutions.

---

† Acessed September 27, 2023. https://jamesdixon.wordpress.com/2010/10/14/pentaho-hadoop-and-data-lakes/.

‡ To follow the history of this story, ask ChatGPT "What are citizen developers in analytics?" and "What is shadow IT.?"

Would anyone really want to get *all* their water from a lake? Dumping raw data into a massive storage system didn't improve corporate decisions at all, but it certainly scaled up the need for data skills. Decision makers seemed committed to keeping their analytic teams locked into data hunting-and-gathering mode.

Let's reset this understanding of a data foundation.

Data Types

The frictionless decision data (FDD) solution takes the opposite approach. It differentiates between three types of data: master data, plan data, and transaction data. Master data creates the *framework* for business alignment. Then the plan data materializes what decision makers *expect* for the future. Finally, transaction activity data from business systems *measures* performance.

I've presented the data types in this order for a reason: It's exactly how *business* decision makers think. Just like your house foundation was built from the ground up, building your data foundation in the right order strengthens the whole solution. But data people make a common mistake of focusing on the largest data sets first when they start building a data solution. Getting the sequence right matters.

To help you recognize these different data types, I'll compare them by four key characteristics:

- Source (where the data comes from)
- Velocity (how fast the data changes)
- Retention (what type of history matters)
- Volume (how much data gets generated)

Master Data

Master data is the logical structure of your business. You can't buy, sell, or build anything until you know *what* you are buying, selling, or building. The products you sell, the customers you serve, the vendors who supply you, the employees who work for you, the projects your teams work on, and the financial accounts you report all form this logical structure.

Systems and reports don't always make this logical structure obvious. Sometimes, it's hard to see the cracks in a foundation without tearing down the whole house. However, the people running a business always understand the structure of their business, even if the data solution sitting on top of it makes it hard to see.

The most pressing question on the minds of many Maxim executives when I joined was about how many customers they served; the seemingly simple task of counting customers wasn't simple. With no consensus about how to do this, the leadership understood that they had a data problem. Depending on who you asked, you might get an answer numbering from a few thousand up to a hundred thousand. This may sound surprising, but high-tech hardware distribution channels are quite complex, products are often generic, manufacturing sites are global, and sales volumes are high.

How could I help the company find a meaningful definition of a "customer" that everyone accepted? For starters, I asked my team and business partners, "What is a simple way to group our customers?" No consensus emerged even on this straightforward question. Not long after, the CEO held an all-hands meeting, updating all the employees on the latest company news. He discussed investments in software, pricing systems, and new teams hired to manage these processes.

"We need to improve our customer service model," he said. "We need to service our Whales, Tunas, and Anchovies more intelligently."

And there we had it: the model for how the company thought about its customers, stated clearly by the top leader. Big fish, average fish, and little fish, all swimming in the same ocean.[§] The customers ranged from the largest tech giants all the way down to college students buying chips off the company website. Not all of them required the same level of attention from the sales team. Using these categories to group the customer data gave the business teams a great starting point.

[§] I recognize that whales are not fish, but from an executive point of view, details are less important.

Then we dug deeper. Many different systems managed customer information, prompting people to ask, "How do we get a single view of the customers?" and "How can we get a single, master database for customers?" All these were good, obvious, next-level questions. We used the data platform to make the data look consolidated because people managed the data in multiple systems, and there wasn't a common view anywhere.

Ultimately, my data team helped the business recognize that two distinct workflows supported the customer master data: first, setting up new customers and, second, determining "who" they were and linking them to a parent entity.

This understanding helped the business teams agree on systems of record for both workflows. Then we killed off redundant databases, changed peoples' data maintenance workflows, and established master data hierarchies for analytics. Maxim went from disconnected confusion to a single customer view that everyone understood. The foundation got fixed while people lived in the house.

Listen long enough for it—how leaders think about the business—and you will hear them describe their business thought framework. That's the raw material you'll need to start building.

Figure 8.1 *The In-N-Out Burger menu breaks down into 45 master data items*

Master Data Characteristics

To help illustrate the different types of data behaviors, let's use the data from my favorite hamburger chain as an example: In-N-Out Burger. We'll start with the menu (Figure 8.1).

I've translated the In-N-Out menu into a table. The menu contains 45 items and 2 "menu types" (items and combos). The items aggregate into six product families and two product lines (food and beverage). Together, all items belong to the "In-N-Out" business unit (Table 8.1).

Master data behaves differently than transaction data, and both behave differently from plan data. They all take on shape, grow, change, and age. Data even retires and gets deleted. Starting here with master data, we'll look at each data type by the four key behaviors I listed above.

Source

What business processes and people generate the data?

The management of In-N-Out Burger decides what goes on the menu; their own strategy and their product development processes define its contents. Their master data gets created before they start selling or buying anything. They don't need to wait around for someone else to supply that information.

Velocity

How frequently does the data get added, deleted, or changed?

Master data changes far less frequently than business activity data. When people go to the drive-thru, they don't care what was on the menu yesterday. They just want to know what it is *now* because they are hungry.

But change the burger recipe without telling them, and you may get some negative feedback. This experience tells us something important about the behavior of master data: It *changes slowly*. Some fast-food chains stretch the limits of this definition, but if you change menu items every day, you might not keep customers very long.

Table 8.1 Fast food menu as master data

ID	Item Name	Size	Menu Type	Product Family	Product Line	Business Unit	Calories
1	Double-double	Regular	Item	Burgers	Food	In-N-Out	670
2	Cheeseburger	Regular	Item	Burgers	Food	In-N-Out	480
3	Hamburger	Regular	Item	Burgers	Food	In-N-Out	390
4	French fries	Regular	Item	Fries	Food	In-N-Out	370
5	Vanilla shake	Regular	Item	Shakes	Food	In-N-Out	590
6	Chocolate shake	Regular	Item	Shakes	Food	In-N-Out	590
7	Strawberry shake	Regular	Item	Shakes	Food	In-N-Out	590
8	Coke	Small	Item	Sodas	Beverage	In-N-Out	130
9	Diet coke	Small	Item	Sodas	Beverage	In-N-Out	0
10	Seven-Up	Small	Item	Sodas	Beverage	In-N-Out	130
11	Dr. Pepper	Small	Item	Sodas	Beverage	In-N-Out	130
12	Root Beer	Small	Item	Sodas	Beverage	In-N-Out	130
13	Iced tea	Small	Item	Nonsodas	Beverage	In-N-Out	0
14	Pink lemonade	Small	Item	Nonsodas	Beverage	In-N-Out	150
15	Lemonade	Small	Item	Nonsodas	Beverage	In-N-Out	5
16	Milk	Regular	Item	Nonsodas	Beverage	In-N-Out	150
17	Hot cocoa	Regular	Item	Nonsodas	Beverage	In-N-Out	130
18	Coffee	Regular	Item	Nonsodas	Beverage	In-N-Out	0
19	Coke	Medium	Item	Sodas	Beverage	In-N-Out	190
20	Diet Coke	Medium	Item	Sodas	Beverage	In-N-Out	0
21	Seven-Up	Medium	Item	Sodas	Beverage	In-N-Out	180
22	Dr. Pepper	Medium	Item	Sodas	Beverage	In-N-Out	180
23	Root Beer	Medium	Item	Sodas	Beverage	In-N-Out	180
24	Iced tea	Medium	Item	Nonsodas	Beverage	In-N-Out	0
25	Pink lemonade	Medium	Item	Nonsodas	Beverage	In-N-Out	210
26	Lemonade	Medium	Item	Nonsodas	Beverage	In-N-Out	10
27	Coke	Large	Item	Sodas	Beverage	In-N-Out	270
28	Diet Coke	Large	Item	Sodas	Beverage	In-N-Out	0
29	Seven-Up	Large	Item	Sodas	Beverage	In-N-Out	260

(Continued)

Table 8.1 (Continued)

ID	Item Name	Size	Menu Type	Product Family	Product Line	Business Unit	Calories
30	Dr. Pepper	Large	Item	Sodas	Beverage	In-N-Out	260
31	Root Beer	Large	Item	Sodas	Beverage	In-N-Out	300
32	Iced tea	Large	Item	Nonsodas	Beverage	In-N-Out	0
33	Pink lemonade	Large	Item	Nonsodas	Beverage	In-N-Out	300
34	Lemonade	Large	Item	Nonsodas	Beverage	In-N-Out	15
35	Coke	X large	Item	Sodas	Beverage	In-N-Out	350
36	Diet Coke	X large	Item	Sodas	Beverage	In-N-Out	0
37	Seven-Up	X large	Item	Sodas	Beverage	In-N-Out	340
38	Dr. Pepper	X large	Item	Sodas	Beverage	In-N-Out	350
39	Root Beer	X large	Item	Sodas	Beverage	In-N-Out	400
40	Iced tea	X large	Item	Nonsodas	Beverage	In-N-Out	0
41	Pink lemonade	X large	Item	Nonsodas	Beverage	In-N-Out	400
42	Lemonade	X large	Item	Nonsodas	Beverage	In-N-Out	20
43	Combo #1	Regular	Combo	Combo	Combo	In-N-Out	1220
44	Combo #2	Regular	Combo	Combo	Combo	In-N-Out	1030
45	Combo #3	Regular	Combo	Combo	Combo	In-N-Out	940

Volume

How much new data gets generated each period?

In-N-Out may take 1,000 hamburger orders, flip 2,000 patties, and issue 1,000 receipts in one day, but there are still only three different types of burgers on the menu. You'll only need three master data records in your database, so the volume of master data storage required will be a small fraction of your overall data set.

Yet companies rarely store data that efficiently. Usually, they duplicate data (and work) by maintaining and storing the same master data in many places. One hamburger might have a lot of characteristics, such as the vendor for each ingredient or the cholesterol content, and this complexity results in clumsy data storage and poor data quality.

Without a plan to centrally manage it, companies unintention-
ally start duplicating master data, exposing themselves to data quality
issues, maintenance challenges, hidden costs, and confused decisions.
An efficient master data architecture (which I'll cover in the next chapter) radically streamlines a business.§

Retention

What kind of "history" should you keep about the data?

Because master data only changes once in a while, the data architect only needs to keep a history of the changes. If you kept daily
snapshots of the In-N-Out menu, they would all look exactly the same
for at least the last 2,000 days.

One of the reasons I (and many, many others) love In-N-Out is
that the menu is so dependable. Do you remember the last time the
menu changed at your favorite burger chain?¶ The most recent change
at In-N-Out was 2018, when they added hot cocoa to the menu.** The
last change before that was 2003, when they added lemonade.

The fact that I can recall those changes says a lot about how much
this knowledge matters to me, but I might be the only person who
cares about it. That's a good way to think about data retention: Consider what you (and your company) will need to remember about the
data after it changes.

It's a good idea to set up "change history" tracking from the start
because configuring temporal storage after the fact is always much
more difficult, like finding cracks in a foundation without tearing
down the house. And you will, for certain, be asked about the history
of master data changes. Like me and my love for In-N-Out, someone
will care enough to raise that question.

---

§ A normal approach to deal with multisourced master data is a Data
Dictionary—a consensus mapping that defines the rules for merging data from
multiple systems.
¶ The hamburger chain Jack-in-the-Box always has some kind of new flavored
burger.
** In-N-Out will give you a free cup of hot chocolate on rainy days.

Plan Data

Plan data—projected or target data about the future—comes in many forms: forecasts, budgets, long-range plans, targets for certain metrics, and so on. Plan data materializes what decision makers *expect* for the future, so it represents the real decisions they've already made about where to invest their time and money.

Yet data teams often simply ignore plan data because it doesn't get generated from an enterprise platform (a "big IT application"). But good business managers don't ignore plan data. It's almost all they think about, like one of my first bosses, Mr. Mori.

When the small manufacturing company I worked at (Silicon Systems) got acquired by the Japanese conglomerate TDK, product failures at customers were common. Something had to change. TDK, famous for VHS tapes, must have felt that their low-tech manufacturing success would translate to high-tech computer hardware, so they sent in Mr. Mori to fix things.††

I dubbed our continual quality issues as "recurring–nonrecurring problems." The products were cutting edge, but our ability to consistently produce *working* products with advanced technology was seriously lacking. The company threw away 40 percent of the product due to quality issues. The goal that year was to make a big improvement … and only throw away 30 percent.

When the results came in, all the managers congratulated each other for achieving this goal, but Mr. Mori was deeply troubled. He came into my office, drew a chart on the whiteboard, and in his broken English asked if I could measure the total value of everything the factory threw away.

"That's easy," I said, "I'll just set the scrap goal to zero. The metric will show *all* the product we're wasting."

What a novel idea. Instead of showing how well we performed compared to easy targets, the metrics showed that we were throwing away millions of dollars in inventory every quarter. Mr. Mori told me

---

†† See the Ron Howard movie *Gung Ho* for a fun story of American innovation meeting Japanese process excellence.

to send this chart to every person on his staff, every week. Sure enough, this scorecard drove a dramatic improvement in factory yields.

Mr. Mori understood that becoming data-driven means knowing what the data *should* look like, ignoring the targets set only to make performance look positive. Why would anyone plan to throw *any* product away? For Mr. Mori, the most important data point was the target. It's the only data the executive truly controls.

Mr. Mori didn't have any idea about the technical side of data management strategies. He didn't need to. He got the core tenet of a business data foundation right: Before you measure anything, you need to know what to measure against, a reference point. Plan data guides decisions. Master data comes before it, and transaction data comes after it.

Where to Manage Plan Data

Plan data builds up your data foundation because it aligns perfectly with the top-level master data you're already supporting in the analytic system. For example, In-N-Out probably doesn't forecast 20,000 individual orders; instead, they probably forecast how many burgers and shakes they expect to sell in total. Managers plan business at a higher level (summaries) than they execute the business (details).

But IT teams usually add friction by ignoring plan data, and business teams add friction by keeping it offline. Both miss a simple fact: Plan data *is* business intelligence. They forget about business strategy and don't realize that they've got spies out there with secret information about the battle, critical information the company needs to win.

To help illustrate the value of plan data in your data platform, just imagine a world where every manager—top to bottom—can see the effects of their decisions on the company's financial plan. And imagine they all could update the plan with new news about the business when they discover it, giving them (and the CFO) instant visibility to the entire profit impact of every decision, analyzable at any angle and at any level of detail. Imagine the power of decisions in setting.

What would it take to make this happen?

This isn't hypothetical; it was the normal expectation of the 400 engineering managers my team supported at Broadcom, people who knew how to make imaginary things reality. It was hard to say "no" to their simple expectation that every decision a manager made would fully and instantly roll up (integrate) into the financial forecast of the company.

Broadcom achieved visibility like this by eliminating the forecasting system itself. Instead of renewing a vendor contract for the latest financial forecasting software solution, we built the forecast inputs *directly* into the analytics system. This innovation removed a massive amount of friction from Broadcom's decision flows. A former colleague (who worked there) told me that when Elon Musk started SpaceX, he refused to purchase software to run the business and instead required his teams create their own. That approach carried over to Tesla, where the company developed its own in-house ERP system, "Warp." Similarly, Broadcom decided that planning was a core skill they already had; the system should conform to the business not the other way around.

Here's why you should do the same thing: When new information emerges about future business, the executive wants to know the impact on the overall business, right now. Without instantly aggregated plan data, business teams start estimating the grand totals offline immediately; people no longer look to the system as the source of truth, and you lose control of the data. Don't lose control of plan data. Learn as much as you can about how to manage it.

Now let's look at how plan data behaves, using our four key characteristics.

Plan Data Characteristics

- **Source**. Plan data comes from the inputs of business managers. Think back to Mr. Mori and how he understood the importance of the plan data. If it's not in your systems already, it's at least in the minds of the leaders. You don't need cutting edge extraction, transformation, or loading tools for this. Simply create a structure for the people in

your company to give you the information—the data—
that they already know.

- **Velocity**. Plan data changes intermittently. Like an
  outfielder in a baseball game, you might not get any hits
  coming your way until the ninth inning, but when the ball
  comes to you, it will be the most critical play of the game.
  Similarly, plan data changes only now and then when news
  comes in. Sometimes it's predictable—you know the date
  of the next corporate review—but other times the changes
  come out of the blue.

- **Retention**. Point-in-time "snapshots" matter most for plan
  data. When fans tune into a baseball game, they usually
  don't care about everything that happened during the game.
  They just want to see the highlights of what has changed
  since their previous watch. Similarly, analysts focus mostly
  on comparisons to previous plan versions. Usually, the
  snapshots synchronize with the business review calendar.

- **Volume.** Unlike low-volume master data, plan data
  grows in lumps. A single snapshot of plan data may not
  be especially large, but analysts need a lot of snapshots
  for comparisons. So, every time a new comparison point
  comes up, the entire data set gets copied (replicated). As a
  result, plan data has a way of piling up in chunks.

Here's some advice: create a plan for getting rid of (purging) old
snapshots. You should also know and communicate the cadence you'll
use for snapshot retention.

Transaction Data

Transaction data is the set of documents that result from normal business activity. Anytime you buy, sell, build, or move something, you're
transacting, and business metrics usually measure these activities. Typically, it's an invoice, sales order, or purchase order, just to name a few.

I'll briefly cover the first four behaviors and get straight to the
value.

- **Source.** Normal business activity, managed in a company's business systems, typically generates all their transaction data. For example, employees fill out a timecard in the HR system and submit it to their manager.
- **Velocity.** Transaction data gets generated fast and steadily, but once it's generated, it doesn't change. That's because a transaction documents something that *happened* at a point in time. Changing that record might not just be pointless, it might also be illegal.
- **Retention** Since transaction data happens at a point in time, you don't need to retain change history; once the transaction gets recorded, it can't change. But since it piles up in high volume, transaction data gets purged at some point.
- **Volume.** Transaction data repeats (and repeats, and repeats). If you've got a good business model, more transactions equal more income. So, you'll need to prepare for enormous data volumes.

How does a good data strategy get the most **value** from transaction data? Every data goal I've described so far in this book aims to make your transaction data "frictionless." FDD gives your company visibility into the *transactions*. It helps people trust the *transaction* data. It allows the *transaction* data to flow freely. FDD unifies your company by delivering *transaction* data to everyone at the same time, in a way that they understand it, with scale and agility.

Transaction Data Agility

If you've never experienced data like this, you're probably unaware of the agility and insight that frictionless data creates. You've probably just hoped the data would allow you to see what's happening in the business right now. But when you've built the framework and reversed the flow, you've created the ability to use transaction data for much more than that. FDD creates an ability to merge and compare entire data sets, and this creates visibility far beyond everyday metrics.

A few examples of data that you might merge and compare:

- **Future demand (or supply).** To get full visibility, you'll need to combine data sourced from some very different sources: open contracts, calculated predictions of renewals, and forecasts of new product sales provided by business managers.
- **Multiple forecasts.** Your sales department forecasts all the potential business if you can supply all of it. But your manufacturing team, knowing all the supply chain constraints, forecasts only what they know they can deliver.
- **Corporate acquisitions.** You just bought a competitor, and the sooner you can consolidate their customer data, the sooner you can capitalize on that acquisition.

In each of these situations, your ability to merge and compare entire data sets, with agility, accuracy, and trust, makes or breaks the value of your data strategy.

Here's an example of how it worked at Broadcom and Maxim. Corporate acquisitions create an urgency to get end-to-end visibility into what's happening in the business. Often, one company acquires another just to get access to their customers. When that acquisition closes, a company that was once a competitor now belongs to you. You acquired all that information for a reason, and the longer it takes your teams to get this consolidated visibility, the more it costs in lost opportunities—opportunities to maximize pricing, margins, offerings, and roadmaps.

Table 8.2 Characteristic behaviors by data type

Data Type	Source	Velocity	Retention	Volume	Example
Master data	Business model	Slow changes	Change history	Low	Parts
Plan data	People's insights	Intermittent change	Points in time	Lumpy	Future revenue
Transaction data	Business activity	Steady activity	Archive after seven years	High	Shipments

Broadcom acquired small startup companies during the 2000s at a break-neck pace; some kind of acquisition was always in progress, at a rate of one a month for an extended time. Acquisitions sound like a great growth plan in a textbook or business talk show, but most companies can't pull this off because they can't integrate companies quickly and smoothly. The first step of a corporate acquisition always comes down to visibility.

For Broadcom to acquire so many companies so consistently meant it knew how to blend an acquired company into every business process at lightning speed. Integrations closed like clockwork. They did this by following the three-level data foundation approach I've explained in this chapter:

- First, set up the acquired company's master data, either in the source system or directly in the data platform.
- Second, consolidate their forecast directly into the data platform.
- Finally, consolidate their business activity with the rest of the business using the data platform, until the business system integrations were finished a few months later.

Both companies were able to see their new, consolidated demand picture immediately after the acquisition closed.

In the next chapter, we'll turn attention to the technical architecture of the FDD solution. First, let's summarize the different data types discussed in this chapter with their behavior characteristics (Table 8.2).

A good data strategist understands why these data types create a firm foundation for corporate decisions, just like the home builder understands what it takes to build a good house. That's just the beginning. With the foundation in place, you're ready to start construction on the house: FDD architecture.

CHAPTER 9

ARCHITECTURE

All in all, it's just another brick in the wall.
— Pink Floyd, Another Brick in the Wall Part 2, 1979

A client sent a team of about 20 data scientists to share their data strategy with me. They presented an overview diagram showing all the system connections and data flows. At the end, I asked the main presenter, "If you need to add some logic to the system, where do you put it? Where do you manage business logic?"

Nobody ventured an answer, not because they didn't understand the question, but because everyone knew the answer: There was not "one place" for logic because they allowed it to go wherever the data scientists felt like coding it, which meant anywhere. And everywhere.

That's the way most data warehouses take shape: tables, fields, schemas, and flows just emerge as projects go along, like a meandering river to nowhere. It looks just like any other database, and you can't even see simple distinctions between different data types. You ask for the design, and the system owner shows you a chart full of technologies. When you're not working toward an overall plan, data usually devolves into a state of nature.

Data architecture is the design that guides your team's thinking about how to build the system. It is not a blueprint, not an answer to every question, and not a technology. The purpose of data architecture is to connect data structures to business outcomes. Just like a home architect understands how people will use the house for their family when it's finished, the data architect understands how the business teams will use the data in decision making for their company.

When I asked the team of data scientists about their plan for logic, I knew this was a quick test to see if they'd made this connection. Business logic connects data to decisions; if you don't have a clear plan to manage business logic, then you're probably not aware of the connection.

Before I lay out how the frictionless decision data (FDD) architecture makes this connection, let's go back in time for some context and understand the history of business data architectures.

The History of Data Architecture

Before data warehousing, organizations just kept their data in the systems that generated the data, systems designed for day-to-day transaction processing. Data warehousing recognized a new purpose for the data by focusing on using that data for decisions, not just recording business activity.

The concept of data "warehouse" architecture traces its roots back to the 1980s, when businesses thinkers realized the need for storing and analyzing large amounts of data and wondered how to get decision making value from it. IBM engineers Barry Devlin and Paul Murphy introduced the concept in their 1988 article titled "An Architecture for a Business and Information Systems." They envisioned a centralized repository where data from different sources would be organized in a way that facilitates analysis and reporting. But the increasing complexity and volume of data made it difficult to retrieve and analyze information from multiple business systems. Data warehousing solved this by centralizing data from various sources into a unified, consistent structure.

This new view implied a new way of organizing the data. Rather than tables oriented toward recording individual transactions, data warehousing saw a common thread through all the data, across all transactions: master data. Master data (discussed in the previous chapter) tied the whole business model together. Data was no longer flat; it became *dimensional*.

Ralph Kimball, an early thought leader in the field, popularized this concept of dimensional modeling in the early 1990s, and his work became a cornerstone of modern data warehousing methodologies.

Shifting Technologies, Shifting Corporate Priorities

This repurposing of the data had important implications for database technologies. While databases that support business processes (like invoicing) perform well for quick recording and retrieval of individual transactions, the analytic database needed to support loading and aggregation of massive amounts of data and support superfast retrieval of entire data sets. These analytic performance requirements—called "workloads" in IT jargon—were completely different from those required by typical business applications.

The practice of data warehousing grew to include technologies for moving and modifying data (extract, transform, load), in-memory analytics, data mining, and visualization tools. These advancements allowed IT departments to do what they do best: copy, move, store, aggregate, and retrieve data faster and more often.

This trend toward data centralization continued through the 1990s, when Bill Inmon developed what I call the "top-down" approach to data warehousing. Inmon envisioned the entire enterprise represented as a normalized data model, with common master data at the center. In this approach, every business process gets integrated and connected, creating the broadest perspective of business activity.

Whereas Kimball's approach encouraged discrete solutions and quick deployments, Inmon envisioned a complete architecture integrating every aspect of the business into a single model. It reduced redundancies and created scale but required a lot more vision and planning.

As the theorists shifted data architectures (like Kimball and Inmon in the late 80s and 90s), corporate priorities also shifted toward analytics. When Broadcom went public in 1998, it was one of the first companies to deploy a business data strategy right from the start. Broadcom's business model was the purest laboratory for these ideas to thrive because leadership already thought of itself as an integrated information ecosystem, so building out this centralized data model made perfect sense to management.

The FDD architecture was born at Broadcom,* and it grew to maturity at Maxim. This new approach extended and advanced data warehousing practices by connecting data architecture with corporate decision processes.

The Layers

Business logic includes anything you do to data that changes it in any way. You can change the message of the data simply by filtering rows, joining columns, adding a calculation, translating a description, naming a table, or by more complex calculations on overall data sets. None of the tools that process data will stop you from doing any of this, anywhere you want. Without a plan, logic (like water) will go everywhere.

FDD creates a plan for logic right from the start by dividing up your data platform into three "layers": replicating, warehousing, and modeling.

- **Replicating (raw).** This layer stores data in its pure, raw form, with no logic or transformation of any kind. No reports or users have access to this layer; it only exists to support the analytic system. We will discuss this layer in depth in the chapter on "Security"; for now, think of this layer simply as exact copies of the source data.

---

* At Broadcom, the architecture was known as "BARS"—business activity reporting system.

- **Warehousing.** The purpose of the warehouse layer is to store all the data in its natural form and make the data easy to find. Like a grocery store structure guides people to the food, the warehouse stores the data with easy-to-locate table names and natural links to the common master data.
- **Modeling.** Users interact with data in the modeling layer. Logic for metrics lives here, with consensus definitions that support all the different teams. The modeling layer also establishes accessibility for every persona: executives who interact with data visually, analysts who explore and matrix data, and data workers who use data mining tools to find new insights outside the standard management metrics.

By keeping these three layers of the FDD solution clearly separated, people using the system understand your logic management plan. Each layer requires a different management focus: different access rules, different organization, and different technologies. Depending on your database, this might mean using separate databases or separate schemas.

Before jumping into the design of these layers, keep this in mind: You'll find all the data types discussed in the previous chapter in each layer. What makes these layers different from each other is the *form* in which they store data, how the data is secured, and where business logic gets applied.

The Warehouse Layer

I asked Serge, the best data architect I know, "What advice would you give to people just starting down this journey?" I knew I was asking the broadest question but also challenging him to boil it down to a simple statement.

I will always remember Serge's answer: "A data warehouse is for data."

Compare this to internet definitions:

- "A data warehouse … is designed to enable and support business intelligence (BI) activities, especially analytics" (Oracle's website).

- "A data warehouse is a central repository of information that can be analyzed to make more informed decisions" (Amazon Web Services).
- "The goal of a data warehouse is to create a trove of historical data that can be retrieved and analyzed to provide useful insight into the organization's operations" (Investopedia.com).

Serge's definition might sound simplistic compared to these experts, but there's a lot more to his perspective than you might guess. From his point of view, the most common mistake people make when setting up a data warehouse is storing data only in the form they want to use it. Business teams seeing the end goal (decision support) would store *only* the data they need for decisions. IT teams seeing the end goal (giving people access to data) would store just what the business teams ask them for.

But Serge understands the simple purpose: A data warehouse is a warehouse. It stores massive amounts of data, keeps it safe, and makes it fast and easy to find what you're looking for.

People today understand the value of warehouses much more than they did even a decade ago. Most of us can't fully appreciate the technology behind the modern warehouse, but we appreciate its basic functions: receiving/unloading goods, staging and storing them, and then preparing the goods for delivery. Imagine if I went to a grocery store expecting a shopping aisle called "Zane's Dinner Menu." That store would work great for a very limited purpose. I'm glad my local grocer (and Amazon) has more vision than this.

Rest assured, the grocery store will address my dinner menu, and the FDD strategy will address my own analytic needs in the modeling layer. For now, let's break down the FDD warehouse layer into four design principles, then I'll explain each one.

1. Store all the data.
2. Store the data in its natural form.
3. Store the data with its natural relationships.
4. Store the data with common master data.

Store All the Data

Take sales orders as an example. Business teams normally look at "back-log" on their reports, meaning the unfulfilled orders only. But if you store only the unfilled orders in your database, you've modified the natural form of the data and limited what you can do with it. If you store the entire set of sales orders in the warehouse—both open and closed—then filtering out the orders already fulfilled becomes a simple operation in the modeling layer.

The situation I've described here, where a company stores data in the form of the end reporting structure (storing "backlog" instead of all sales orders) is a real example and a very common data architecture mistake. Many large global companies have this type of problem, but the only thing a senior manager knows is that their decision data is not working; it's not frictionless.

You never know what future questions you'll need to answer with the data, so keeping full data sets with their natural relationships in place prevents future rework.

Store the Data in Its Natural Form

On a business document (like a purchase order), you'll see a list of items with information about each item, like the item number, description, quantity, and price. You'll also see information about all the items, like the shipping address and payment terms. When you store data in its natural form, you store two tables: header and detail.

You'll find more complex examples than this in a real implementation, but this simple point gets skipped all the time. Teams think in terms of the metric they're working toward and end up flattening the data in many ways.

Store the Data With Its Natural Relationships

Storing the data in its natural form preserves the relationships that the source system created. The "header and detail" example above is a simple example of this. But natural relationships also include integration—the way different data sets relate to each other.

For example, sales orders and shipments naturally relate to each other. When a shipment goes out, the remaining sales order quantity goes down. When a delivery gets received, the remaining purchase order quantity goes down.

Here's where a data strategy produces incredible leverage for a company. Creating these natural relationships is a core function of business systems, but that doesn't always happen; system migrations, acquisitions, or business process gaps disrupt things. When the natural relationship is working properly, the warehouse layer naturally supports that link. But when it's not working properly, the warehouse layer can easily create that link as a stopgap. Setting up business systems to work right could take a while, but management visibility can't wait.

In either case, your data warehouse should mirror the natural relationships between data sets that the business process expects. This business awareness of how the data really works will protect you from creating new technical debt.

Store the Data With Links to Master Data

Here's where the data warehouse adds scale. You've already centralized master data, creating the common thread that links every business process in your company together. Now, in the warehouse layer, adding the reference to that master data makes it easy to find what you're looking for. Instead of searching for data related to a part number, you can find all the data associated with a product line.

Here's a simple summary: Your data warehouse is not a spreadsheet, and the design of your data management system is not the same as the format of your pivot table. Instead, your data warehouse supports the needs of the entire company. Your data warehouse is for data.

The Modeling Layer

Now I want to introduce you to the most exciting (from an analyst's point of view) part of the FDD architecture: the modeling layer. The modeling layer contains the tools, security, dimensions, and metrics that make data understandable to every decision maker in your company.

Only two innovations occurred in the 30 years since data warehousing took hold in corporate enterprises: pivot tables (perfected by but not invented by Microsoft) and visualizations (invented a century earlier and perfected by Tableau).

"Pivoting" data is simply an interactive matrixing and rematrixing of the data, helping the analyst see aggregate totals at any level they choose. This invention suddenly turned analysts into data explorers. Interactive visualizations did the same thing for charts and graphs. Business decisions mostly use aggregate data, so these tools were a great step forward for companies trying to become data-driven.

But people still struggle with the data. They still spend most of their time downloading data, adding logic and formulas, creating master data hierarchies, and cleansing data. That's the gap the FDD modeling layer fills.

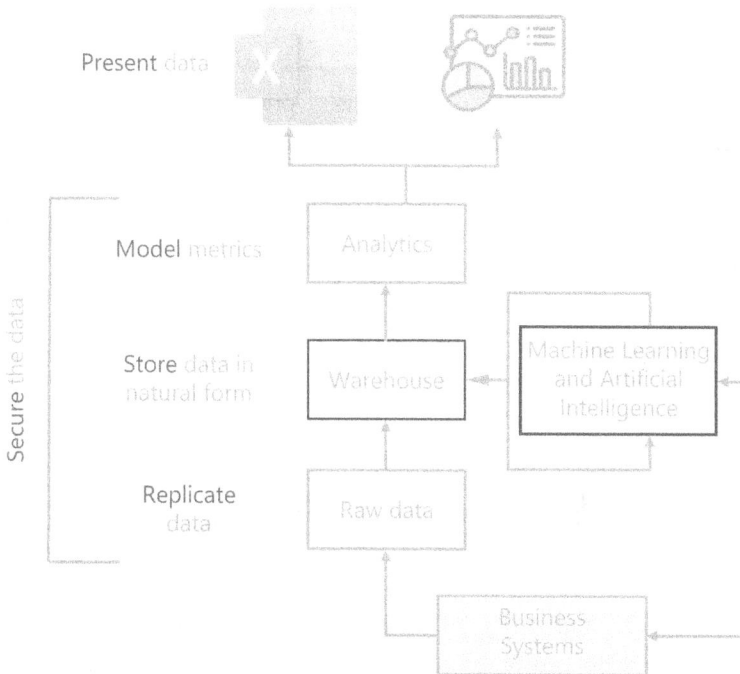

Figure 9.1 *FDD architecture defines specific uses for each layer of the system and managing logic*

Three components make up the modeling layer: database models (cubes), pivot tables (Excel), and visualizations (Tableau, Power BI, or any visualization software). The modeling layer presents one data set through these three analytic tools (Figure 9.1).

Database

Database "cubes" contain the dimensions, calculations, and metrics people use for analysis. If you're picturing a Rubik's Cube in your mind, that's right: You can twist the data into just about any combination of colors.

Cubes "preaggregate" or index every *intersection* of the data; if you view a cube with an Excel pivot table, you can look at the aggregate data across three dimensions (columns, rows, and pages). These indexes put the data into the computer's system memory, which makes queries extremely fast. When you think back to our discussion of master data hierarchies in the previous chapters, you see how this structure creates a powerful way to explore all the intersections.

How many different analytic models does your company need? Generally, one for each major business process. It works this way because a business process (like moving "orders to cash") uses the same master data dimensions across all the steps and data sources within it.

Use the company's standard P&L statement as a quick reference to see those processes. In semiconductors, there were five models:

- **Demand:** customer, product, and margin analysis
- **Sales pipeline:** customer opportunities
- **R&D pipeline:** project analytics
- **Headcount:** people analytics
- **Financials:** General Ledger (GL) account and cost center

You might need different models for a different industry. For example, an entertainment business would likely use a model that analyzes productions by genre or ratings by platform. A health insurer would focus on policy utilization (engagement). In all cases, the analytic model relates to financial statements.

The core master data tables (like customers and products) are also stored in the modeling layer. This illustrates how the three parts of the modeling layer work together.

- A data worker connects (joins) directly to the master data through SQL.
- An analyst pivots the data with their spreadsheet.
- Executives view it with a standard BI report in their web browser.

In this way, a single table with all customer master data streamlines everyone's reporting and keeps the data uniform across all reports and reporting tools. FDD makes the data accessible for any use.

Pivots and Dashboards

In the FDD architecture, analysts connect pivot tables and dashboards directly to the database (either cubes or tables). The data remains in the database, and the tools only "present" the data to the user. No data moves out of the database, except what's visible on the charts or displayed on the pivot table. The cube enforces all permissions at the database level, so people will see the exact same data in whatever tool they use to view the data.

FDD is here to set these tools free to do what they do best: help people understand their data. It's almost the whole point of the FDD architecture: I want to set pivot tables and visualizations free. People shouldn't have to build logic in them, they shouldn't have to use them to hunt for data, they shouldn't have to download millions of records into them, they shouldn't have to build hierarchies, and they shouldn't have to integrate data sets.

Use whatever tool you want to explore the data. The data is ready for it. Set the analysts free.

By now, you've probably recognized that the strategies presented in this book will impact the way your company organizes its data teams. Let's take that topic head-on with a discussion about how to centrally operate these functions.

CHAPTER 10

ORGANIZATION

Someone's always playing corporation games,
Who cares, they're always changing corporation names.
                    —Starship, We Built This City, 1985

After sharing my data strategy ideas with a friend—a Human Resources executive who'd worked at Amazon, General Motors, and Bank of America, three companies with three completely different business models—he immediately asked me the same question that might be going through your mind:

Should you centralize or decentralize your company's data and data strategy?

He wasn't surprised when I said "centralize." Of course, he immediately pointed out that Amazon, likely one of the most data-driven companies on the planet, decentralized their data teams. After all, Amazon has so many business units in so many different fields, why would you possibly want to store all that data in the same place? What he didn't know is that I knew a business affairs analyst who had worked at Amazon. And this decentralized approach caused the exact friction I'm talking about in this book.

Even at Amazon.

I'm sure you've recognized by this point that everything I've laid out so far assumes a centralized business data strategy. Now, let's take this question head-on. Leaders like my friend often state simple, binary, zero-sum dilemmas, like: "Is it this, or is it that?" They're not looking for your answer, they're looking for your thought process.

My answer? "It depends," I said.

With semiconductors, you have a single business model serving a lot of different markets. The automotive industry is similar in this sense. Amazon, on the other hand, combines lots of different business models into their platform: retail, streaming, cloud services, and so on. The better you understand the business model of your company, the better decision you'll make about how to centralize your business data strategy.

Rather than two opposite alternatives, align on the business models. If units of the company operate independently, then don't force them to share a data solution. But don't use this as an excuse not to centralize; instead, find the balance where a centralized data strategy delivers the scale and alignment the business needs.

To help you find this balance, first I'll explain the core benefits of centralization to your decision processes. Then I'll give you some pointers about how to decide the right balance for your company.

Centralization Creates Visibility

Centralizing your data team helps them get visibility to the overall flow of data through your company. They get to see the big picture, which helps everyone. I call the scope of that visibility the "domain," meaning a defined area of knowledge and expertise. A "domain architect" is someone who has both visibility and control in a technical area of the system.

People with the most technical knowledge—those who know how everything really works—usually don't manage people. But they add a critical influence and governing control over the architecture.

Centralization helps senior team members use their visibility to find new ways to improve the overall strategy.

Domains and Subdomains

This idea of domain architects also applies to lower-level areas, as illustrated by the chart on Figure 10.1 below. Four subdomains make up the overall "data strategy" domain: business process (how the company works), applications (how the software supports the business), data (how to manage the information), and technology (how the platforms enable the business) (Figure 10.1).

When the experts in each domain belong to a single team, these domains start *working together*. The value of centralizing your data team isn't mainly about cost reduction or controlling priorities; the real benefit comes from removing friction between people in these knowledge domains. A decentralized team simply cannot collaborate between these domains like they would as a single team. They'll always have disconnected, incomplete, competing solutions. That's friction at its finest.

The domain chart looks like an org chart, but instead of defining people's titles and supervisory authority, it shows a hierarchy of *technical expertise* that divides up these subdomains even further. It

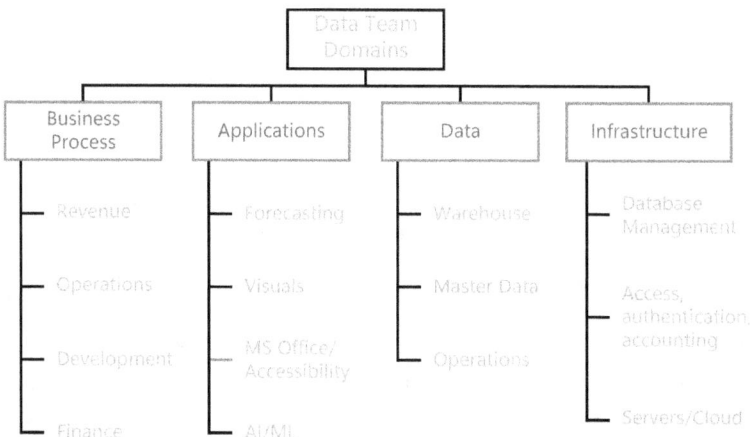

Figure 10.1 **Align the data team by domain to create scale and sustainability**

communicates ownership and relationships between areas of technical decision making. You don't get promoted to the next level of an architecture domain; instead, you earn the respect of peers when they look to you as the expert.

Outcomes

If you've understood how all the different parts of the FDD solution fit together (like master data and transaction data, or warehousing and modeling), you start to see the *interdependent* nature of the entire architecture. The same applies to the organization: creating a team structure like this makes the entire team interdependent on each other. The centralized model I'm sharing helps the team and the strategy to move in lock step.

There's no way everybody can understand every detail of technical systems. If you want to get the most out of a system, people need to trust each other with technical decisions. At Maxim, everybody on the data team became an architect in their specific knowledge domain, giving them respect from peers, decision ownership, and room to grow their influence. Trust grew as the team challenged each other's ideas and discovered new innovations together.

Maxim's leadership understood the technical teams in this framework, and it led them to create new job titles and new growth paths for key individual contributors in the data team. That gave the architects more influence in the organization, and they made fundamental improvements (like making data move faster) to the data practices of the entire company.

Centralization Right-Sizes a Data Team

Centralizing a data team helps you dedicate the appropriate number of people to the data practice for your company. When people all over the company spend their time on data work instead of making business decisions, it costs a lot more than a centralized team. IT people call this "shadow IT" like I described in the "Foundation" chapter.

But the real cost of *not* centralizing is in the missed opportunities for analytic insights. When business analysts spend less than 20 percent of their time on analysis, who knows how many insights they've missed?

Both Broadcom and Maxim managers saw this leverage and decided to transfer headcount from their own teams to my data team. In both cases, the data team increased to double digit headcounts. From the outside, this seemed like a large cost center, but the opposite was true: Business teams across the company became far more efficient when trusted, accessible decision data was served to them with all the technical expertise of IT.

What's the right size for a data team? I'll offer a simple starting point to help you evaluate if you are anywhere in range. According to a Harvard Business Review study,[1] a company with a well-aligned enterprise system architecture spends about 18 percent of its IT budget on "shared data." By applying an industry appropriate rate of IT spending for your company (like 2%), you can translate it into a headcount number. A manufacturing company with $1 billion in revenue works out to about 15 people dedicated to a centralized data team.

Change Management

Consolidating a centralized team from existing teams won't be easy. Resistance won't come from top management or the data workers themselves; both benefit from consolidation. It's the middle managers who need convincing because they might lose influence. Here are a few ideas to make this easier on everyone:

- Start by identifying critical business reporting flows that are linked directly to an individual, single point of failure. Help that person improve and stabilize their work and let the business teams experience the benefits. Do this, and middle managers will realize that this individual could do even more for their team if they were part of the data team.
- Make a case to align data functions within the IT department itself. Companies that don't know how to

align the functions of a data platform tend to separate
all the different parts of a data team into different IT
groups. For example, the team in charge of moving data is
supervised by a different manager than the team in charge
of managing master data.

This creates friction-filled IT workflows where one IT person
must open a service ticket just to get another IT person to do work.
Remember this: The more help tickets IT people create for other IT
people, the less IT is helping the business. Don't create mindless workflows like this that kill agility.

Centralization Clarifies Roles

To make your data strategy truly frictionless, you'll need some people
on the data team who focus entirely on the business process domain
and not technical work. These people know how the business process
should work and find ways to align the systems and the data with that
process.

What's the biggest complaint you usually hear about IT teams?
They don't understand the business. And it's usually an accurate assessment. But the data team works face to face with everyone in your
company, helping them use and understand the output (data) of every
process and system. Centralization creates space for the data team to
include this important capability.

One of the most valued members of Maxim's data team was Truman, a programmer who understood the company's sales data better than anyone. I asked him to take a Business Integration Analyst
role and step away from technical development work. His entire job
became explaining data to business users.

Faced with a new question, Truman was just as likely to convince
the business teams to change the way they did their work as he was
to recommend a change to the system. For example, when business
managers asked him to add logic to sales order reports to estimate a
new kind of discount, Truman redirected them to an unused feature in

the contract management system, a solution that gave more complete data and didn't require any business logic changes.

Separating Motivations

Separating development work from business process work makes your team a lot smarter because it aligns their motivations with their responsibilities. Software developers solve problems by writing code; if they say "no" to a request, they fear perceptions that they're just being obstinate. But because of his job role, Truman and the business teams were incentivized to find solutions without changing the system whenever possible. He could say "no" to a request because he found a way to solve the problem without writing code, and it sounded helpful. He was free to recommend the best solution with or without a system change.

Truman became so trusted that business teams didn't think they could survive without him. When I approved his request for a seven-week vacation to Mount Everest (something that rarely happens in both mountain climbing and data jobs), I think the business teams were afraid there would be nobody around to say "no" to their bad ideas. People don't like hearing "no" to their requests, but they trust you a lot more than someone who just says "yes" to everything. Truman returned from the Himalayas with some great stories, picked up right where he left off, and everyone relaxed.

This "Business Integration Analyst" role on the data team was the X-factor that made both the Broadcom and Maxim teams so impactful for the company and the overall IT and Finance functions. Including this role on the team might seem like a luxury, but it's really at the heart of a team driving frictionless data.

Centralization Creates Clear Roadmaps

I've made the case that all data is in some way financial data. Let's take that idea one step further: Starting with financial data means you're starting at the *center* of your company. Every business activity gets reflected in the financial data, somewhere, somehow. Your company may have a lot of interesting data, but not all data projects bring alignment to a company. You need a rational approach.

A frustrated manager at one company told me, "If our executives could just make up their mind about what metric to measure, my job would be a lot better, and we'd get a lot more done. Instead, I'm tracking a hundred metrics, and they're still always asking for something new." Another client was spending a lot of time and money cleaning up the contact data on the sales leads. Yet the company didn't have any process at all to assign customers to their parent company.

I told them, "Cleaning up the data for customers who *might* buy your products sounds like a great idea for the sales team, but understanding the customers who *already* buy your products matters to everyone."

How can you move past the kind of friction that always prioritizes the urgent and the "nice to haves" ahead of the important? Rather than taking random requests from business teams to build reports, a data strategy centered on financial data follows the logical progression of the P&L. The top line becomes the most important line, and analysis of revenue and margins takes priority. Eventually, you get to the bottom line: profitability.

Finding Balance

Your own business context determines how much centralization you'll need. I'm not offering you a blanket rule—you'll need to make decisions that work for your own setting. Here are a few ways to find the right balance of what teams and systems to centralize.

Compare the Master Data

If the master data used by one part of your business is completely different from the others, both in content and structure, then you might be better off with separate solutions. For example, one part of Amazon manufactures electronic gadgets, and another sells streaming services. Very little of their product master data overlaps.

Compare the Source Data

If the source of business data all comes from the same place or in identical formats, then you might benefit more from centralizing. For example, you might build trucks in Michigan and sedans in Kentucky, but the shape and form of the business data are virtually identical no matter what kind of vehicles you manufacture. If you've got two different teams managing that data, you could get more leverage from a consolidated approach. Eliminating redundancies like this doesn't just make you more efficient, it also leads to more alignment.

Compare the Business Models

If your company consolidates multiple business models into a single forecast (plan data), then you might benefit more from a consolidated strategy.

For example, financial service companies sell many different types of products within their banking business, but they view banking as a single business unit, so centralizing adds value. Semiconductor companies often sell software and design services not just chips, but they forecast them all together. On the other hand, Amazon cloud services operates entirely separate from Amazon's online retail and video business.

I'm not saying that every metric is a corporate-level metric. A local branch manager might measure their location differently than the corporate office. But alignment and visibility depend on centralization. Look at the way your company plans and forecasts overall financial results, and you've probably found the right groups for centralizing the data strategy.

Now that we've thought about the team organization, let's turn our attention to how to position that team to respond to the constant changes and business opportunities your company faces. How can your data practice help the decisions in the entire company become more agile? We'll cover this next.

CHAPTER 11

AGILITY

I can solve the world's problems without even trying.
—Styx, Too Much Time on My Hands, 1981

If you search online for the meaning of "agility," you won't find any mention of Information Technology. Instead, you'll get a list of "10 Moves That Make Working Out Feel More Fun," which proves that we all know agility matters, but we also agree that working out is not fun, and becoming agile is a lot harder than we'd hoped. Some of the suggested exercises:

- Lateral jump
- Two jumps forward, one jump back
- Squat out/hop in
- Single leg forward hop
- Lateral lunge

- Side-step toe touch
- Skater with toe tap
- Plank jack
- Wide to narrow push-up
- Quick feet

Unfortunately, all these exercises require *balance*, something I just don't possess. I can't stand up on a surfboard, for example. As much as my friends tell me what I'm doing wrong, no amount of practice will fix that problem. The minute something unexpected happens—like a breaking wave—I fall right off. I've learned that surfing requires both knowledge (how to surf) and balance (not falling off).

It's like that with your data strategy: The business situation constantly changes, forcing you to quickly adjust without falling off. Executives decide to reorganize their product lines because they want to target new end markets. The price of a commodity rises dramatically, affecting all products. A new opportunity to provide services (in addition to products) becomes the top priority. A new accounting rule requires different revenue reporting methods. The list goes on.

If you can't deal with change quickly and easily, your data strategy won't survive. You'll either say "no" to changes or destroy the system with shortcuts. Your ability to respond to unexpected circumstances—without wrecking the architecture—makes or breaks your data strategy.

That's agility: the ability to move quickly and easily and still stay on course.

Nimble Practices

Just like Google suggested a set of exercises you can do to help develop your own agility, I'll give you three ways to develop agility in your data strategy. These three practices will put you, your team, and your system in a posture to nimbly respond to the constant changes facing your company: **maintain** data hierarchies differently, **accelerate** the cadence, and **triangulate** the decision processes.

Maintain Hierarchies Differently

The system where you maintain master data hierarchies directly impacts your team's agility. Two practices make your solution agile: aligning maintenance with ownership and storing hierarchy data at the right level.

Companies reorganize themselves constantly: realigning products, regrouping customer service models, changing the reporting relationships of employees, or adding new services, for example. When management considers a reorg, they want to see what the data will look like after the changes. Analysts usually mock up the changes offline, on spreadsheets, a lengthy, error-prone, nonrepeatable exercise that requires a project plan and a lot of co-ordination. Worse, it's always guesswork. If the data looks good on the spreadsheets, they decide to move forward with the changes. What the data really looks like when people update the data in the business systems remains to be seen.

It shouldn't be that difficult.

Yet this approach is so common that most business teams never consider that they could use the system to model the changes. They assume the friction is normal. Reorganizing the data could happen immediately, across all the systems.

Here's how to remove that friction. First, align maintenance with ownership. Make sure the person (or team) who owns decisions about how the business data should roll up also controls maintenance of that data in the system. Master data hierarchies are *decision data,* and analysts make all the decisions about what should change. Forcing analysts to hand off that data maintenance to a team that's busy with transaction processing adds only friction not value.

Instead, you can manage many of these values (like product line names and relationships) directly in your data warehouse. This is a counterintuitive approach from an IT perspective (a data warehouse should not originate any data), but it optimizes the workflow, optimizes the data architecture, and creates agility.

Second, store hierarchy data at the right level. Let's say that every product belongs to one product line, and every product line belongs to one business unit. If you store the business unit name as a characteristic of every product, you multiply the amount of effort to maintain the business unit values and expose the potential for mistakes. If you have a thousand part numbers, you'll need to update all of them just to change a single relationship.

You might be surprised how commonly this simple design approach gets ignored, resulting in systematically bad quality data. Companies stumble on this all the time, storing values at the wrong level, and then add more programming code to fix the problem. Software developers call this "WET" (Write Everything Twice) programming.

The most efficient way to store hierarchical data is to store it at the level decision makers normally think about the relationships. In data warehousing terms, storing hierarchy data in separate tables and with relationships to other master data is called a "snowflake" design. When you set up master data hierarchies with these practices, you've changed the game completely. Instead of a month-long project to evaluate, plan, and reorganize the business, a single data change updates every report and analytic tool overnight.

That might seem like *too much* agility. But it reduces risk by increasing visibility to all changes; after all, only one data point changed. More importantly, business teams will use this agility to their advantage. Instead of trying to predict the profit margins of a newly reorganized business, they'll use the analytic system to find the result. Managing hierarchies like this takes full advantage of the agility built into centrally managed master data.

Next, let's talk about how your solution can make daily metrics more agile.

Accelerate the Cadence

Watching a large band in a parade captivates the audience because they're seeing a few hundred people playing different instruments, while marching, all fully synchronized. Most of the time the drum section plays the street beat, known as a "cadence." It keeps everyone at their pace, headed in the same direction. Everyone knows what to do and what comes next.

Like a marching band, metrics and data also move to a cadence. The frequency at which people receive reports, their metrics update, and their data gets retained ("snapshots") all communicate a rhythm and set expectations about how things work. Most companies already march to some kind of information rhythm; decisions move at a pace, some daily, some monthly or quarterly, and some annually.

Here's a funny example: Lots of companies issue a "flash" report to management. The report looks different depending on the type of company, but they all give it the same name. The "Flash Report" always shows the metrics that the executives want to see most frequently. It's often someone's full-time job to assemble the report. One company I advised had a little department supporting this report, but they could only get it done three days a week (Monday, Wednesday, Friday), more like a dimmer switch than a flash.

That's the point of the flash report: to establish a reporting cadence. Two simple cadence practices will help you instill agility into your data practice: adopt a daily cadence and avoid real-time analytics.

Adopt a Daily Cadence

I've found a surprising amount of confusion in data practices about the pace of reporting data. One company was loading sales order data to their reporting platform on the first Monday of each month. Sometimes that day was six days after the end of the previous month. Business data users would forget about this timing and constantly ask each other why the data was wrong.

A daily cadence sets a clear pace for the overall data practice. You might think that a daily report of the same metric is overkill but think about all the benefits:

- It eliminates debates about what time of day the data is "as of." You'll be surprised how much alignment this simple decision creates.
- It helps the data team recognize data issues sooner, and it helps them focus on reliability. Delivering data daily means that you get 365 chances a year to perfect the process.

- It creates an environment where *incremental improvement* is normal. The data teams at Maxim and Broadcom typically made hundreds of system and data enhancements every quarter, without disrupting any business processes. There's no such thing as a "big bang" in an agile data practice. Changes that data users think should be easy really are easy. That's agility.
- It gives management the ability to react to near-term business changes almost instantly.

Avoid Real-Time Analytics

Business analytics always requires *context*. If you want to make sense of data—if you want to draw any conclusions—the most important data is the reference point.

Here's an example. We know the Sun is 93 million miles away from the Earth. That seems enormous until you learn that the Milky Way is about 100,000 light years across. We find value in data when it expands our understanding, which requires a reference point.

When an executive looks at a metric, they usually compare it to the previous period or the plan for the period. This implies a natural "cadence" or tempo. While "real time" might mean that a metric is updated as of three seconds ago, to an executive, a daily report is effectively "real time" because a day is the smallest bucket of time she uses in her thought processes.*

With today's technologies, IT teams really can deliver data to the analytic desktop in real time. But just because you *can* deliver data in real time does not mean you *should*; instead, take a normal approach and validate the use cases before delivering solutions. Accelerating the cadence like this creates agility by making it easy to react to changes.

Let's take it one step further, by linking the thought processes of different business teams. I call that "triangulation."

---

* Some might ask if daily reporting is even required. Most decision metrics require larger time buckets for context. But a daily cadence creates the most flexibility for unforeseen analytic needs.

Triangulate Decision Processes

As a new business idea progresses from first concept to generating real revenue from real customers and products, the details in the data grow. Businesses make plans along the data hierarchies, but they execute the business at the bottom level. You'll need an agile data strategy to link these thought processes (planning) to the detailed business process (executing). That's "triangulation": systematically linking related business processes that use different levels of business data.

Every company recognizes that they should link these processes somehow, but almost no company links them with data. Instead, they try to link them with reporting solutions. That rarely works—it requires so much data mapping that it's never repeatable.

Let's walk through an example. When you design a new product, you give it a generic name, but when you build and ship it, you create lots of different models or stock keeping units (SKUs). This involves data from many business processes, at different levels of detail: Return on Investment (ROI) planning (with generic product names), designing (also generic), selling (some generic and some SKUs), manufacturing (SKU), and shipping (SKU).

Let's assume you've successfully implemented the frictionless decision data (FDD) master data strategies, and your product hierarchy data allows you to summarize lower-level business transaction data and join it to the higher-level planning data.

Now for triangulation: Your project management system, where you manage the work to build new products, tracks work by generic product names. The CRM (customer relationship management) system also uses generic product names to forecast new product sales. Do they create this master data independently? You can change this to a workflow—generic product IDs created in the project system should flow directly to the CRM system. Do this, and you've connected the investment process with the sales process. Enforce this relationship with all the FDD master data management capabilities.

When master data hierarchy values flow across planning systems like this, plan data and business transaction data naturally link, eliminating the need for data mapping altogether. With this friction eliminated, data-driven decisions radically accelerate (Figure 11.1).

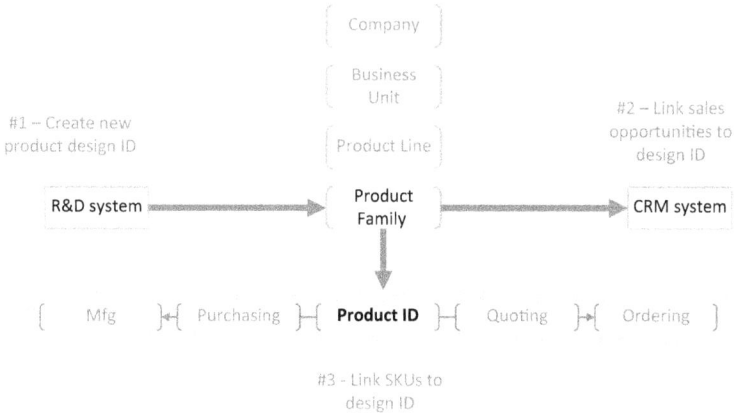

Figure 11.1 Key business processes rely on hierarchy data; FDD connects them with business processes instead of reporting systems

The 00001010 Commandments of Data

I've spent this entire chapter helping you understand how the FDD framework delivers agility. But sometimes simple rules help clarify the spirit behind them. So, I developed this short list of dos and don'ts that should give you a feel for what you're getting into. These rules won't help you make great data decisions on your own; you'll need this whole book for that. But the rules will help you think about why they follow naturally from the strategy. And they'll also give you a safeguard if you haven't fully grasped the whole architecture yet.

Clumsy Data Practices

1. Never use reports to do something a system already does.
2. Never give access to raw data.
3. Never build logic in reporting tools.
4. Never mask bad data with logic (always fix data at the source).
5. Never break the link between an operational change and a metric effect.

Agile Data Practices

1. Always measure the whole before measuring the parts.
2. Always store the data first instead of skipping to metrics.
3. Always store data as journals.
4. Always enforce cell-level security.
5. Always use hierarchies (instead of logic) to align business definitions.

Have fun with these commandments. See if you can explain what data management strategies they connect to. When you start grasping the FDD strategy, you'll start thinking of your own commandments. Congratulations, you're reached data nerd status.

Now that we've covered the FDD approach to a data strategy (the "why") and the FDD solution (the "what"), we're ready to move to the operating model—the *practice* of managing data. Just knowing how to build a good data foundation isn't enough to change the strategy of a company. You'll need to use influence to do that. I'll help you translate your knowledge into influence next.

PART 4

Influence the Business

President Eisenhower said, "Plans are worthless, but planning is every-thing." I think he was explaining that, however much planning you do, you still must fight the battle.

That's the point we've reached in this book. I've exposed the prob-lem of how data friction affects all your decisions. I've explained the concept behind Frictionless Decision Data, that you need to reverse the flow of data and decisions. And I've shown you how to build the framework that supports a frictionless data model.

Now it's time to fight the battle. Here's what you'll find.

Refactoring. IT teams developed a lot of bad habits over the last 20 years, and that gave them a bad reputation: nobody thinks of them as strategic business partners.

But now you've learned that a data strategy can change that. And just like your desire to get skinny doesn't make you lose weight, your colleagues will need to change some of their habits if they expect to become data-driven. In this chapter, I'll give you four key habits IT teams need to break. CIOs who do these things will become that outlier in corporate life, the IT leader who is also a trusted business partner.

Security. You might think of data security in terms of limitations and consequences. I want to reverse that idea and show you how the FDD security approach leads to real business partnerships. You're giving leaders control over their data. Most of them have never heard of or seen a partnership like this. Combined with the overall strategy, this chapter will help open doors across your company to work together with you and your team.

Accuracy. I've talked a lot about establishing trust in data. Now, I'll show you what that looks like in practice. In this chapter, you'll find three specific operational practices you can implement in your data platform to ensure that the data aligns with financial data. Then I'll show you how to make data quality measurement an everyday partnership with the teams you support.

People. I've shared a big vision with you in this book. Now let's take it to the team. That team is the face of IT, the first responders to every issue and every opportunity. After managing data teams for twenty years, I'll share with you what it takes to value, lead, and inspire a good data team. I'll help you connect the vision with the work.

I hope I've convinced you up to this point of the importance and impact that a good data strategy has on a company. Now I want to translate that knowledge into a real, strategic partnership between you and the business. That's a new experience for IT leaders. When you connect the dots between the data and the decisions, that's real influence.

CHAPTER 12

REFACTORING

Time for jumpin' overboard. Transportation is here.
—Talking Heads, Burning Down the House, 1983

The Chief Technical Officer of a large software company called me looking for help. Their company was replacing home-grown business systems with a new vendor-managed enterprise software. Two years into the upgrade, the business problems it was meant to solve ... hadn't been solved

"Things are just as fragile as always. Manual work is still manual. People hold the systems together. And nobody can tell me how it's supposed to work," he told me. "We're stuck, and I'm frustrated."

I asked him a bold question: "Why are you, the CTO, asking me about this? What happened?"

He laughed. I was right, something had happened: Two CIOs were fired over the last three years.

"Look, you understand how your business works," I said. "You understand how to create demand, how your company generates revenue. But the business data flowing through your company barely corresponds to this. Show me how you think about the business, and I'll map every system and process to that. You've got a data problem not a systems problem," I said.

"You're right, that's it … but how good are you at change management?" my friend wryly asked.

He was right, IT needs to change.

Everyone knows why you need IT: They manage your systems and data. They keep the systems up and running. But does that mean they're just a utility? Does a successful CIO just keep the help desk response time under three weeks, or should they make a difference in the way a company manages its business? Can IT people contribute to the strategy of a company, or are they just candidates for cost reduction?

The term "refactor" comes from IT lingo. It means that you need to rewrite the application code (how a system runs) without changing the function (what the system does).

That's the technical definition. IT managers use this word all the time, especially on PowerPoint slides. But "refactor" really means the system is breaking down, barely running, and if we don't rebuild the system from the ground up, it will stop working altogether very soon. Things are getting bad.

Why is IT broken? Why does IT need to refactor itself?

It's because of the data. Data connects business to technology. We need a new kind of IT leader who understands what it takes to connect them. We need a new kind of IT that knows how to make data useful for business decisions. To make this happen, let's look at three old habits that need refactoring.

Refactor #1: Stop Creating Reports

A friend challenged me to count the number of shirts I own. It was a little embarrassing to admit that my giant, walk-in closet housed about 150 shirts, most of which I'd never worn. I gave up about half of them, simply by eliminating the shirts that no longer fit. My friend delivers excess clothing to people in need, so they went to a worthy cause.

Yet when I see a cool t-shirt, I feel compelled to impulse buy it and reload my closet with stuff I'll wear once (maybe) and then never wear again.

Many data teams have the same problem as me with my t-shirts: Every business question looks like an opportunity to add another report to the library. Yet the more reports they create, the more likely they don't have a data strategy. Just like my friend did for me and my closet, I want to challenge your perspective about how many reports you really need.

If you accept my argument that decision processes usually follow a repeating structure, then it follows that you only need a small, limited number of reports to run a business. Don't resign your company to perpetual report writing. Instead, let's refactor your data and analytics approach from a "reporting" process to an "analytics" process. How do you do this?

Report proliferation usually results from the failure to distinguish between personas and use cases. Think about the three personas we discussed earlier: service staff, analysts, and executives. If you want to avoid creating a new report for every question, start by recognizing who is asking the question. Executive and operational people use standard reports; when they ask a data question, don't create a new report. Improve the reports that you already have. If the question comes from an analyst, show them how to use the data system to find what they're looking for.

The data model creates the *capability* to investigate any question, even those questions that nobody has asked yet. That's the opposite of reporting. It's the framework—the data structure—that analysts use to look at data. This framework includes the dimensions, calculations, and measures you apply to the data.

Here's an example of an analytic model. Broadcom called the customer order data the "3Bs" because there were three components—bookings, billings, and backlog. Everyone who used the data understood this complete picture of customer order data. They understood that today's backlog equaled yesterday's backlog, minus yesterday's billings, plus yesterday's new orders (bookings). All executives received reports in this structure, all analysts used a single analysis tool to explore it, and all operations people used the same language when they discussed the data with executives and analysts.

This simple analytic model reflected an understanding of how these three data sets (new orders, existing orders, and shipments) related to each other. That understanding didn't come out of nowhere; IT took a business understanding of the data and applied it to the way they stored, processed, and presented the data. If they didn't start with that business awareness, IT would have just created a new report for every view of customer data that the business asked for.

This combination of business, data, and technical awareness helps you stop creating reports.

Refactor #2: Stop Taking Shortcuts

People who write reports make a common mistake by creating logic or writing code that only reproduces data that a business system already produces. Shortcuts like this never satisfy. Business teams, rightly so, ask for the metrics they need for decisions, and IT teams usually respond by creating logic to calculate those metrics. But writing more report logic always handcuffs the data and reduces agility. Instead, they should respond by giving the business teams *data*.

Here's a rule of thumb to help your data team avoid creating logic when they shouldn't. I call it, "Measure the whole before measuring the parts."

Take "shipment" data for example. The broadest measure of shipments is the revenue number that appears in your P&L statement.* Measure it in dollars, not just units. If you include all the data in your system that's needed to match that total, you'll know for sure that you captured all the data you'll ever need. Most metrics are just a matter of categorizing data in different ways, so if you capture everything to

---

* This doesn't account for shipments you make to yourself, but you shouldn't analyze that anyway.

begin with, you're a lot less likely to try and fill data gaps with logic. If you count the total number of trees in the forest first, you'll be more confident about your counts of fir trees and spruce trees.

The Maxim IT team once missed this approach with one of their own core metrics: data storage capacity.

A new CIO was starting with the company soon, so I tried to guess the first question he'd ask me. "How much data storage does this company use?" was my best guess. After a few months of research and learning, we got it all added up: The company stored about 3.2 petabytes of data.

More detailed questions about the types of storage we used followed some more expensive, some less expensive, some hot, and some cold. Soon, discussions about how to reduce storage costs, which were going in circles up to that point, started moving forward as management could make reliable estimates of the savings that might result from operational changes.

About six months later, I happened to mention to the new executive that I once measured the total data storage of the company. Surprised, he told me, "That's the question the CEO asked right when I joined the company!"

One company worked for many months to create metrics from one of their core data sets. Every time the IT team completed one metric calculation, they realized that they needed more logic to get the numbers right. When I got my hands on their analytic data, I saw that they had added hundreds of columns to the data set, just to display all the calculations. They didn't realize that they could have avoided almost all this logic by simply capturing more data from another part of the business process.

If you don't start by capturing all the data from a business process, then you will be forced to create more reports and more logic until you finally (hopefully) see everything. Missing this approach is a lot more common than you'd think because business teams usually don't ask for it.

It takes "data awareness"—understanding the end-to-end business data flow—to see the value in measuring the whole before measuring the parts. So, start at the top. It will help you to stop creating logic.

Refactor #3: Stop Aimlessly Moving Data

Think about it: If all business activity gets recorded in a single system, then you don't need to move data at all. But diagrams of data pipelines at most large companies look more like spaghetti. How can you ever unravel it?

Once when I was tasked with setting up a new, consolidated reporting system, I successfully got a powerful, cutting-edge server setup in an East Coast data center. Some of the key data we needed sat on another server, on the same rack, in the same data center. But due to unrelated security concerns, the two systems weren't allowed to exchange data. The work environment was a little tense, and employees were hesitant to make any system changes, so my request to connect these two adjacent servers went in circles for months.

The business teams, meanwhile, didn't care at all about the IT policy. They just wanted to make business decisions, and they needed the data *now*.

Moving the data from the East Coast to the *Texas* data center didn't require any approvals at all. And since the California data center was already connected to the Texas and East Coast data centers, my team successfully got the data moving to the new server by sending it on a daily trip around the United States. It only took a few hours, not the shortest physical path, but clearly the shortest approval path. Mission accomplished.

Well, not so fast. My rule of thumb on data integrations—take the shortest path and don't make any stops along the way—remained the goal, so we pursued approvals at every level. In the end, I pasted a map of the United States onto a single PowerPoint slide, explaining to the IT security executives that our data made a 7,000 mile cross-country round trip journey every morning, just to move the data a few feet to the server right beside it. The slide worked, the change was approved, the security policy got changed, and the integration got optimized.

The more data that moves between your systems, the less you've integrated your data. How can you stop all this movement? The key is matching the *business purpose* of a data movement with the appropriate technology.

To help you unravel all the data movement you've already got, you'll need to understand the different approaches to make sure you're using the right one in each situation. Three simple categories help explain the technologies that move data: messaging, batching, and mirroring.

Messaging

Messaging, the most common type of data movement between business systems, moves data one document at a time and always makes sure to get a receipt, just like the messaging app on your phone. The IT term for this kind of data movement is "synchronous," like a handshake at every step in the process of moving the data.

If you've ever sat at a restaurant, just watching your food sit on a counter waiting for someone to deliver it to your table, then you understand how a poorly integrated system hobbles a business process. This illustrates a common mistake IT teams make when moving data: making stops along the way. If the business process expects synchronized data movement, don't substitute another approach.

Batching

If you like baking cookies, then you know everything you need to understand about batch data movement: All the cookies go into the oven at the same time. It also means that if you make a mistake, like setting the temperature too high, you're going to burn the whole batch. If you promised the kids that the cookies would be ready in an hour, you'd better be right, or you'll have everyone waiting.

Batch movement is the exact opposite of messaging; it's asynchronous and aggregated. It moves a large set of records all at once. If you're using batching to move transactional business process data, you're using the wrong technology. But batch data movement is a good fit for analytics use cases because it's periodic by nature, just like the decisions it supports.

Your spaghetti-like data landscape likely uses mostly batch data movement already because it's the cheapest, easiest way to move data.

But for this same reason, it's the most common failure point in your data operations. So, make sure you have a way to monitor all the batch processing and recognize failures before users do. Establish benchmarks for when you expect jobs to complete and use these references to proactively improve the system performance.

Mirroring

I stopped flying Southwest Airlines cross-country for the same reason IT teams should stop moving so much data. It took me a while to realize that saving a little money isn't worth having to stop in Denver and Chicago every time I want to fly to New York. More take-offs and landings create more potential for delays. The best way to make a one-way flight to New York from California is nonstop.

Database mirroring works like messaging, except that it only goes in one direction. There's no receipt acknowledgment when the data moves from its source to its destination.

Mirroring data makes it perfectly real time and the most reliable and the most efficient way to move data in a modern analytics architecture. Companies rarely achieve this level of integration because their business applications rarely share the same infrastructure. But even when they do, IT policies may also create resistance to this solution. Replicating raw data like this to your data platform makes the data you get from other systems clean and reliable, but it also creates a temptation for business teams to misuse that raw data and let it get into the wrong hands. You'll need good data governance policies to make this approach safe and secure.

This brings us to the critical topic of data security. IT also needs to break bad habits that give everyone access to everything. Let's talk about an approach to security that actually helps a company make better decisions.

CHAPTER 13

SECURITY

Just hold on loosely, but don't let go
If you cling too tightly, you're gonna lose control.
            —38 Special, Hold on Loosely, 1981

One of the first things I needed at my new job was access to the company data. Snooping around a while, I determined which systems supplied the data used on most of the existing reports. I asked a new friend in the hallway what I should do for access, and two minutes later I got an email from him with the user ID and password. That was quick!

The reason it came so quickly was that *everyone* who used the data knew (and shared) the login credentials. This system contained live, active transaction data for many software apps and storage for much of the company's business system data. For years, people kept adding whatever data they wanted to it. I slowly discovered that those credentials were hard-coded in thousands of reports and interfaces.

I know this example sounds extreme, but it's a true, uncomfortable, repeating story. In this chapter, I'll discuss the causes that lead to a situation like this, the risks it creates, and how frictionless decision data (FDD) governance addresses the risk. Think of this chapter like a confessional booth: It could embarrass you or make you overconfident in your current situation, but in either case, transparency matters most. Use it to honestly assess your current strategy.

The purpose of all data security is to make certain that people have complete access to *only* the data they need to do their job. Helping your company make better data-driven decisions means getting more data into more people's hands, but if you let that data get into the wrong hands, you've failed. You might conclude that your mission to make data accessible competes with your responsibility to make it secure.

How can you resolve these competing goals?

Without a good data strategy in the first place, you can never give people the data they need for their job and prevent them from seeing data they shouldn't. You'll always grant too much access or too little access. Usually, companies make both mistakes.

Part 1: No Data Strategy, Too Much Access

Some companies without a data strategy in the first place default to granting access to entire tables or databases (giving access to everything) or restricting access to individual reports. This leads to more bad data practices: creating more tables and reports simply to limit access.

Other companies without a data strategy grant access to reports or screens. While at first this might seem to severely limit access, eventually people get access to lots of different reports, effectively seeing all the data.

Neither approach gives people just the data they need for their job. People get frustrated by the situation and finally ask for access to everything. It's common to see a security solution where the "All Access" group has the most members.

Cell-Level Security

Good security—scalable, granular, and understandable security—starts with logically structured data. You've got to secure the information *inside* your data tables, which means securing rows and columns of data, not just tables. I call this **"cell-level security"**: enforcing access at the intersection of rows and columns within data tables.

About a year after that first encounter with the shared access situation at Maxim, the FDD solution was in place. When a new product line manager (PLM) started working at the company, they got assigned a data access role that matched their job. Every report and data cube they looked at automatically filtered the data to just the products they were responsible for, including past, present, and future revenue data.

Then, a management "flash" report showed up in their inbox every morning, showing them key metrics for their own product line, in the same format that the CFO and CEO received for the whole company. Everyone knew they were receiving the data at the same time, from the system, and they understood that the data they explored online was the exact same data set.

Because the system filtered every report and query to just the right data for each user, the IT team didn't need to create many reports. Everyone used the same report and the same cube.

The PLM got this access the day they started their job because the Business Unit General Manager approved their access. When he approved it, the GM also assigned the new PLM access to the product line they would support.

When the PLM role was set up in the first place, the data owners (Cost Accounting VP and the Finance VP) had approved access to pricing and costs for everyone in the PLM role. They approved this because they knew that all the PLMs would only see their own product line, so there wasn't any risk of exposing total company numbers. All this forethought meant that the PLM got access to all the prices and costs for all their products, automatically.

I'll explain more about how this worked technically and administratively in a moment. Before we jump into that, think about the effect it had on the way people used data in decision making:

- Collaboration improved as communication aligned up and down the management hierarchy.
- Decisions accelerated because nobody spent time trying to understand how their data fit into the overall totals. The framework made that clear, and people had the data they needed for their job from day 1.
- Overall data security improved because less data got exposed to people who didn't need it.

Managing Access

Four FDD capabilities combine to deliver security like this: role-based access control, data cataloging, identity management, and user monitoring.

Role-Based Access Control

The shared login situation I described at the beginning of this chapter didn't arise simply from technical limitations. The owners of that data did not end up in that situation because they didn't know how to administrate usernames and passwords. No, they failed to enforce security because they didn't know what data their users *should* see. You can't enforce a set of permissions that you haven't defined in the first place.

You'll need an administrative process to define, approve, and enforce what people in different job roles ("personas") should see. IT people call this "role-based access control." I'll use the examples below to show how this works.

The FDD role definition matrix defines ownership like this:

- **Role owners.** These people approve new access requests. They also review the full membership of the role periodically to identify people who've changed responsibilities recently. Role owners also "assign" specific permissions to individuals, like naming which product line someone should see.

Role	Role Owner	Role Members	Dimensions (rows)				Data Scenarios (pages)				Measures (columns)			
			Product Line	Product Family	Cust Region		Billings	Orders	Forecast	Units	Prices Mary Miller	Costs Doug Davix	People Greg Green
Product Manager	John J.	11	Assigned	Assigned	All		Yes	Yes	Yes	Yes	Yes	Yes	No
Sales Rep	Sally S.	14	All	All	Assigned		Yes	Yes	No	Yes	Yes	No	No
Product Line Analyst	Bob B.	7	Assigned	All	All		Yes	Yes	Yes	Yes	Yes	Yes	Yes
Operations Manager	Gina G.	10	All	All	All		Yes	Yes	Yes	Yes	No	No	No
HR Manager	Tina T.	3	None	None	None		No	No	No	No	No	No	Yes
Cost Accountant	Walt W.	5	All	All	All		Yes	Yes	No	Yes	No	Yes	No

Figure 13.1 FDD secures data at the intersection of job roles, dimensions, and measures

- **Data owners.** These people decide what job roles should get access to a metric (like prices or costs), across all reports, visualizations, and databases.
- **Permissions.** Together, role owners and data owners decide what dimensions, data sets, and measures each job role should see (Figure 13.1).

That's the administrative framework for security. There's nothing technical about knowing who should get what data, it's entirely a business decision. But the framework for these decisions helps the business owners make security decisions at the granularity they naturally think about access.

Next, you'll need to enforce those permissions, starting with cataloging the data you've got.

Data Cataloging

A data catalog is exactly what you'd expect: an index people can use to identify the contents of your data. But I want to advance this beyond the Wikipedia definition. The common data catalog simply lists all the database objects (like tables, views, users, and so on) but doesn't tell you about the data itself.

Take another look at the role-based access matrix above. The FDD approach creates the structures you need to *catalog* data; it categorizes all the data in the system. This three-dimensional approach—dimensions (rows), scenarios (pages), and metrics (measures)—tags every data point in the entire system with an owner. Just like management makes decisions along the vertical master data hierarchies, people also think about what data they need for their jobs along the same hierarchies. In the FDD security model, master data hierarchies provide the data values you use to assign permissions.

Now you know who should see what, and you know what data you will secure. Next, you need to identify who exactly is connecting to the data.

Identity Management

Identity management simply means knowing the actual person using a system. Most data security difficulties start with just recognizing who is doing what, similar the shared login situation that I found on my first day at work. When a login isn't tied to an individual, it could be anyone using it.

People should be free to use whatever tool they want to visualize, pivot, or simply report from the data. That's a core tenet of a frictionless data strategy. To make that possible, FDD security requires that the *database system* can recognize who you are (your identity) and what you should see (your role). Pushing security enforcement to the lowest level of the system makes FDD "tool agnostic" for end users.

For example, an analyst wants to pivot the data with Excel; they simply connect their spreadsheet directly to the database. The executive uses a dashboard to visualize a data trend; that dashboard also connects directly to the database. The hands-on data worker? They might use an SQL tool to mine data directly. Whatever tool these people use, they'll get the same data.

Most business analytics tools run on Microsoft Windows, so the most integrated platforms will often use Microsoft Active Directory security, which allows your database to recognize logins and let the operating system handle the authentication. If you're using a different platform to manage logins (or not managing identities at all), then connecting identities to assignments and the data might require more technical steps, or alternatively, it might limit your ability to make your system "tool agnostic."

User Monitoring

Usage monitoring is simply keeping track of all the report and data usage by login name, including what data the person used, what report they used, when they used it, and how long it took them to retrieve that data. Keeping usage activity like this helps when (if ever) you need to do forensic research. Data exfiltration—downloading data and taking it outside the company—is an important example of this. We'll cover that next.

But the practical value of monitoring people's data usage is that you can service them better. Knowing what data people use most often is a great tool to help a data team focus on performance, quality, and improving the data sets people value the most.

Exfiltration and Spreadsheets

Even if you implement all the FDD controls I've described here, you still face the most common data security risk: exfiltration. When people (or thieves) take the data with them (outside the boundaries of your network), you've lost control of the data altogether.

People almost always use a spreadsheet to take data with them. No matter what you do or say, the data will always end up in a spreadsheet somehow. But you can't stop people from using them. Trying to take spreadsheets away from analysts is like trying to take guns away from people: You know how much risk it creates, but for analysts, taking their spreadsheet way threatens a fundamental right.

Microsoft Excel is the gold standard for spreadsheets. You, the analyst, might use another spreadsheet if your company requires it. But when your job performance depends on tools, you always want the best tool. So, from this point forward, I'll use "Excel" instead of "spreadsheets" for the discussion.

Think of the issue like this: People make most decisions based on data they see in PowerPoint. Here's how that flow of data normally works in most companies:

1. IT stores data in a database platform.
2. IT loads the data into a reporting system.
3. Analyst views the data with an online reporting tool.
4. Analyst downloads the data to Excel.
5. Analyst summarizes the data in PowerPoint.
6. Analyst presents the data to an executive.

Downloading data to Excel is not a corner case at your company. No, it's an everyday, multiple times per day activity for every analyst. Massive amounts of data already flow out of your system to Excel just because people want it there. You've got to stop this flow, and taking Excel away from people will never get through Congress.

Here's the FDD flow:

1. IT stores data in a database platform.
2. Analyst views data in the database with Excel.
3. Analyst summarizes the data for PowerPoint.
4. Analyst presents the data to an executive.

By embracing Excel, allowing people to connect their favorite tool to the database models, the day-in-day-out activity of downloading data suddenly becomes unnecessary. People let the database do the work of storing lots of data and aggregating it for decisions. The only data they copy to PowerPoint is the answer, the summary information they share in a presentation. The FDD architecture integrates Excel rather than tolerates it.

This flow of data down to desktops and possibly outside your company might scare you. And it might be worse than you think. Giving access to raw data supersizes that risk; I'll expose that next.

Part 2: The Case Against Raw Data

Rather than a comprehensive inventory of all risks, I'll highlight one foundational concern. I will make a case for never allowing any person or system access to the raw data that you capture into your reporting system. Raw data—the unaltered copies of data from source systems—is your most important information asset and yet the part of your architecture that can wreak the most havoc if mismanaged.

Raw Data Bypasses Security

Good security—scalable, granular, and understandable security—starts with logically structured data.

Data security (the assignment process I described previously) aligns with the master data hierarchies, not the raw data. Thinking back to our hamburger chain example ("Foundation" chapter), a decision maker needs access to "food" or "beverage" data, a characteristic of the data known only from the master data hierarchies (decision data) at the core of your dimensional model, not the raw transaction data.

If granting access to raw data is your current approach, you might as well just admit you have no plan to secure the data at all.

Raw Data Subverts Business Logic Alignment

If you only give people access to the data processed through your data management system, you've created the opportunity for everyone—all data consumers—to benefit from common reporting logic. But the minute you allow report writing from raw data is the same minute you've lost the ability to get the company aligned on a single set of business logic.

Raw Data Kills Your Ability to Catalog Data

Data "lineage" is the process you establish that helps people understand where it came from, what it means, and where it gets used. Good data teams create "data dictionaries" (for example) as a regular habit, making it clear to people who want to know what logic you used to arrive at a result. That's especially important for master data. Transparency like this develops trust.

Haphazard approaches to cataloging data don't work; without a structured plan to manage the data, your ability to identify the data, know where it's used, and who owns it will always fall short. Exposing raw data to users just skips this best practice.

Raw Data Performs Poorly

Useful analytic queries run fast. Allowing users to create reports from raw data might seem practical, but you're simply not doing anything to improve the normal experience of the people using the data. Your network speed and the patience of your analysts will all be tested to their limits.

That's why databases feature "indexing." By adding an index to a table, the queries people run don't have to search through every record in the table. Indexes make queries go faster. They also make loading raw data to the table go slower. Business systems typically store data relationally (OLTP[*]), and analytic systems store data "hierarchically" (OLAP[†]). These two different approaches to "indexing" provide preset addresses for finding data quickly. Indexes help queries avoid searching all the records in a table to find the data you want.

Relational storage (OLTP) makes it fast to find any single data record, and it also makes writing a single business transaction to an enormous database incredibly fast. Oracle dominated the business world by perfecting this feature.

On the other hand, summarizing data to find the total number of hamburgers sold in a month at In-N-Out Burger requires capturing a huge amount of data rather than a single transaction. It's a different purpose for the data, a different person asking that type of question, and (importantly) a different type of indexing and database technology to retrieve that data at the speed they expect. Creating a technology that does both activities—writing transactions and reading aggregates—and doing them both superfast have eluded database scientists for decades.

Even expensive database solutions (like SAP's HANA) live under these constraints. They do a great job of mirroring and then quickly aggregating data from its ERP system in real time, but the database fundamentals haven't changed. Most of the data (like point-in-time snapshots) people need for analytics doesn't live in an ERP system and doesn't need to be processed every minute or even every month. Any good enterprise database system supports these capabilities.

---

* Online transaction processing.
† Online analytic processing.

Raw Data Is Not Time-Based

You'd be surprised how many senior executives maintain their own personal copies (snapshots) of reports, not trusting the system to support this. Every analytic decision process uses other reference data for context, which always means storing data snapshots.

Allow access to raw data for reporting, and you'll encourage everyone to keep their own data snapshots. Doing this will create shadow data storage throughout your company and expose new data risks.

Raw Data Kills Self-Service

My grocery store introduced self-service checkout stations a few years ago, which helps me get in and out of the store a lot quicker. But chaos would ensue if the store manager decided to make all of us shoppers unload the trucks and hunt through the pile of food for our groceries.

Self-service always means making things easier for someone to do themselves, and using raw data for reports is just like sending your users to the unloading dock to get the groceries. This point may sound counterintuitive but think about it: Someone, somewhere, must aggregate data for decisions; a good self-service model requires more structure, not less. Just giving everyone access to the raw data makes everyone's job more difficult. It's not a real strategy.

Business Partnering With Security

Here's some advice. Managing security like I've described here creates a lot more value than you might realize. It makes everyone's job easier. It reduces risk. It catalogs your data.

Shortcuts like the shared password situation I described at the beginning of this chapter always add risk and create a lot more work in the long run. That password got hard-coded into thousands of reports, and those reports got used to feed data into more software applications. Millions got spent to sustain—and undo—those data dependencies.

But more importantly, when you take a business-oriented approach to security like I've described, it opens a door for you to become a true business partner. That happens when you identify a Vice President as an overall data owner and give them control over who gets to see an entire data set. At that point, they realize you're helping them manage *decisions*, not just data. Don't miss this opportunity.

As I write this in a Duluth, Minnesota coffee shop, I am reminded of how often people simply make security the last consideration when they set things up; the Wi-Fi password just shared with me by the barista is "coffee123!" Effective security doesn't take shortcuts.

The same is true for accuracy: It requires a good business process. I'll explain that next.

CHAPTER 14

ACCURACY

One day it's fine and next it's black.
　　　—The Clash, Should I Stay or Should I Go? 1982

I learned a lot about the importance of credibility from emails discussing the Broadcom cafeteria. Anyone with a laptop at the company could send an email to all the employees, and when someone got sick on the salmon, engineers felt no hesitation using this access to share their thoughts, immediately, with everyone in the building. A full afternoon of company-wide emails questioning the credibility of the cook (one of the finest in Orange County) would follow one person's bad reaction to the fish.

Data has a lot in common with food: Everyone consumes it, but few understand the process that delivers it to their desktop. If there's even a whiff of tainted data, people stop trusting the entire system. The *reputation* of the data makes all the difference.

When people in your company see data that they don't understand, the way they react shows how much they trust your data strategy. Do they immediately assume all the data is corrupt? Maybe the report accurately shows bad data coming from the source. Do they consider that maybe their own understanding of the data is wrong, or do they immediately conclude the cook made a mistake?

A good data team earns trust over time by demonstrating accuracy, consistently responding to inquiries, and continually working to make the data more understandable. It's hard to earn trust and easy to lose it. In this chapter, I'll show you how to gain that trust and keep it.

Financial Accuracy

Data trust doesn't happen by accident, it results from a plan for measuring and communicating accuracy. I'll explain three specific ways to make financial accuracy a core part of your solution:

- Link all data sets to financial master data.
- Embed reconciliations (comparisons of one set of data to another) into the analytics solution.
- Store data as journals.

First, use financial master data to link all other data sets. In accounting lingo, financial master data is known as the "chart of accounts" or general ledger "chart fields." This includes the company codes, cost centers, account codes, and other fields required for a journal entry.

Every business transaction maps to a certain combination of these fields, so when you start with this data at the center of your solution, you're then able to link every metric to it at some level. Links to financial data might be fully automated or completely manual, but in either case, you'll need to understand how the data gets posted. You will learn how every business transaction works.

For example, the shipping system generates an invoice for every shipment, which also generates a ledger posting. But the customer information only exists on the sales order. So, to get financially accurate numbers for the shipment data and include the customer information, you'll need to link the journal entry to the invoice, the invoice to the shipment, and the shipment to the original sales order. That's more work than simply creating a report on shipments. But when you do this, you've created a financially accurate data set that is useful not just for the shipping team but also for the sales and finance teams.

Second, reconcile all data. "Reconciling data" means that you compare one data set to another and resolve the differences.

I call this process "certifying" a data set. Decision data (like customer information) is a lot more detailed than financial data, but their numbers should match in total. You should "embed" comparisons like this into your solution by creating a report that finds the differences, then research and resolve all the differences every month. When you complete this process each month, notify people that the whole data set is qualified and ready for use.

At Maxim, one of my team members named Anne took this on as a personal challenge. She centralized this business function of reconciling data and made it part of the regular analytic data processing. Instead of everyone auditing the data themselves, she provided accuracy as a service. The reconciliation controls she created got built into the financial controls of the company.

Soon, Anne was explaining to the accountants the situations when they were out of compliance with revenue recognition policies and to business managers how to get credit for their sales. She created so much confidence in financial accuracy that even external investors relied on reporting directly from the system. Anne created trust with her ability to explain every data point when asked.

If you're an IT person, reconciling data shows people you're thinking like an accountant. People trust accountants more than IT people, so that's a good thing.

Third, store data as journals. In the 15th century, Luca Pacioli, an Italian monk and mathematician you've probably never heard of, changed the world with an invention you almost certainly know:

double-entry bookkeeping.* One of Pacioli's basic rules, "debit what comes in and credit what goes out," seems intuitive in our day, where it's common to use data to describe the world.

Although this innovative approach to business thought changed the world six centuries ago, there's a good chance it hasn't taken hold yet in your local data and analytics solutions. I'll make a case here that journal entries aren't just for accountants, it's also a framework for all analytics.

The beauty of accounting data is that it tracks all the ins and outs, which you can then summarize to get the balances. Two core financial statements—profit and loss, and balance sheet—are summaries of what you did (the activity) and what you have (the balances). You can apply this idea to all your data sets: If you store the data underlying your analytic models this way, you're ready for any question about the summary data. Soon, you'll start seeing how storing data in a journal format exposes the most possible information about changes in the data.

Let's take the number of people working at your company for example. "Headcount" is the "balance" of the employee count at a certain point in time. You'll want the ability to compare today's headcount to what it was yesterday (or any prior period) and to the plan for that period.

During the day, you hired some people, some people left or transferred, others changed their names or titles, got raises, and so on. This activity—the ins and outs—all happened during the day, and the activity explains how the headcount balance at the end of the day increased or decreased from one day to the next. Headcount isn't always understood as financial data, but it certainly impacts your profitability, and

---

* Pacioli published "Summa de arithmetica," (meaning, summary of arithmetic, geometry, proportions, and proportionality) where he introduced the concept of debits and credits. His innovation created a structure for the way business transactions had always (messily) worked. By standardizing business thought with journal entries, he launched modern accounting and removed friction from everyday business decisions. This work was so influential that he's now referred to as the Father of Accounting.

storing it in a financial format creates the most insight into what's happening.

Here's another example: open sales orders. The number (and amount) of unfilled orders at a point in time is your "balance." Your balance of unfilled orders may be larger or smaller, depending on business volume. You'll want to compare the open order balance today to what it was, say, a month ago. At the same time, you took new orders and shipped some existing orders, all part of the periodic activity. Storing data in a journal structure creates a natural "bridge" between periodic balances—you'll always be able to explain how much you've got now and how you arrived here, removing the mystery about why the numbers changed.

Don't just use journaling for financial data, use it for everything.

Exception Reporting

Exception reporting implements the business process for building trust in the quality of your data, as discussed in the "Trust" chapter of this book. It closes the loop between data issues seen on reports and the business systems where the data originates. A "business rule" always links these.

Exception reporting is a simple, three-step workflow to fix data problems: When someone sees bad data, then (1) define it, (2) measure it, and (3) fix it.

I'll explain these steps.

Step 1: Define the business rule. If you want accurate data, you need a definition of "good" data. Here are some examples:

1. The data is not missing.
2. The data matches a list of acceptable values.
3. The data is not out of date.
4. Data that should be the same in different systems really is the same.
5. Data is not higher or lower than related data.

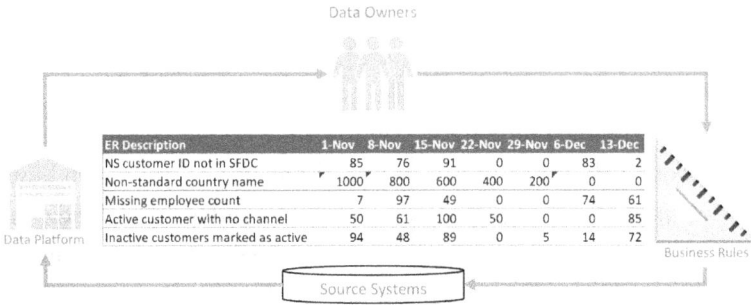

Figure 14.1 Exception reports close the loop between data seen on reports and the systems that manage the data

Whatever happened to make the data wrong is also something we'll need to resolve, but the data must get corrected either way. Better now than later. There's no "acceptable" level of error; all bad data should be fixed.[†]

When you create an exception report, you've defined a new business rule. Just few words or a short sentence, like "Customer IDs in Salesforce but not in SAP" (like type 4 above), is all it takes; if you can't state the rule in plain English, then maybe you need to simplify the rule or define more than one rule.

Step 2: Measure data quality. That business rule (written in plain English) translates into simple code, selecting the bad records. The system runs the business rule and emails the records to the business owner. This process helps data owners keep their eye on the ball, and it also helps management keep score by logging daily a history of the number of errors for each rule.

Let that daily email be an incentive for people to fix data; if they fix it, the emails stop. Use that daily error count to help the data owner track their progress. The overall data owner also gets to see the progress; the HR director, for example, gets to see all the data errors in her area (Figure 14.1).

---

† Herein lies the difference between a metric and an exception report: Metrics have a nonzero acceptability threshold.

Step 3: Correct data at the source. When you put this process in place, people fix data where it should be fixed: at the source. The people who own the data fix the data.

Eventually—hopefully—bad data stops, emails stop, and the exception report shows zero every day. Why? Because the data owner developed a complete understanding of the broken business process. That knowledge translated to a systematic change, ensuring accuracy right up front. The feedback loop going from the decision process to the business process has completely closed.

Data Quality as Culture Change

Maybe people in your company tolerate bad data, blaming it on the system, like it's not their fault, and the root cause is somewhere upstream. Broadcom's CEO was right to see this as a culture issue, like I mentioned in the "Trust" chapter. People shouldn't tolerate broken things (or bad data); he wanted a company where people are willing to deal with an issue and show up every day to fix it until there's a permanent solution.

When people see bad data, they learn to hear a business rule, and they know what to do when they hear it. Instead of complaining and instead of just fixing bad data when they happen to encounter it, you want them to record a business rule. Recording a simple business rule helps you do a lot more: It creates the opportunity to assign an owner, the person responsible for fixing the data. And this should always be a person.

At Maxim, data owners began to recognize the value of documenting their business rules this way and started asking for more. It didn't take long before there were hundreds of exception reports. Even better, the IT team used many of these documented business rules to permanently fix the root causes. If you establish these processes I've explained for accuracy, you've become a good traffic cop. You've instilled discipline in your company's data management.

I've made the case throughout this book that a data strategy is not just a technical solution, but it's also a management strategy. Outcomes like trust and agility aren't just a description of your system, they're mostly a description of your people. So, I'll finish this book by going back to the people, the most fundamental part of your data strategy success. I'll show you what it takes to manage a data team well.

CHAPTER 15

PEOPLE

Light up your light tonight,
I wanna see you shine.

—The Alarm, We Are the Light, 1984

It was a sunny Sunday morning in January 2021 when I got an urgent call from a Texas employee. He'd just learned that the Philippines staff were having trouble shipping orders. The system had slowed to a crawl, and the inventory was piling up. The products waiting for shipment were headed to automotive customers, the most pinched part of the red-hot, postpandemic economy. So (apparently), my team successfully brought the American supply chain down to its knees, and I felt personally responsible for all the problems everyone was hearing in the news. I escalated the issue to the highest urgency and got the whole IT staff on a virtual call.

When it comes to an IT disaster, just recognizing the situation is usually the biggest challenge. Outages usually unfold like a slow-moving train wreck. IT people habitually blame most problems on "user error"; they struggle to see the big picture, and admitting there's a system-wide failure often takes a lot longer than necessary.

But I had data. I accessed a metric on the system response time, by hour, over the previous seven days. I discovered that, although the IT team thought the problem started when the shipping clerk called that Sunday morning, the problem really began a day earlier before the shipping team started work. When it comes to understanding data, context matters most; the situation was a lot worse than my team knew.

I called my best friend, who works as an insurance adjuster, and asked him what he thought I should do. You've got to start somewhere when you're in over your head.

"Whenever I have an unsolvable computer problem," he said, "the first thing I do is reboot. IT always tells me to flip the switch off and on. It usually works." he said.

Nobody had a better idea. Around 8 p.m., with no root cause identified, I suggested we give the global supply chain system a reboot. The whole team disagreed with me, even though they all were my subordinates. It took a lot of trust (for me) to work through all the alternatives first and then (for my team) to perform a global system reboot. Sure enough, the system restart worked.

When it comes to managing a data team, dominant technical skills aren't enough. *Business vision* inspires a data team because it's so rare; they already know the value of the data they manage, and when someone comes in with an actual plan that connects their efforts to business outcomes—and they see it work—it helps them trust you.

Part 1: Explaining the Value

Most companies think of IT departments as a service organization. I've heard many IT and Finance leaders ask, "What does it cost IT to 'keep the lights on'?" tacitly admitting that they see IT as a utility, as a cost center that should be managed to the bare bones. And many parts of IT really are a pure service cost that supports the business rather than driving business strategy.

But a data team isn't your typical IT team. They don't fall neatly into the common IT categories like applications and infrastructure (discussed earlier). Data teams work directly with real people solving real problems every day. And more people work with data than work with the systems themselves. They're the face of IT.

A startling example of this happened when Broadcom was moving to a new shipping system. When it began as a startup in the late 90s, the company used an accounting software application called "Quick-Books Pro for Mac." That desktop software was effective until revenues reached eight figures. The company installed an enterprise-level software package to manage the business, and the IT team spent several months getting the new system ready. Part of that readiness included moving all the customer data into the new system. The night before the new system was going live, I received the final list of customers to be moved; the next morning, we'd start shipping to these customers.

Data analysts (like me) often "profile" data. They want to learn about the shape and form of the data, not just the metrics. The IT term for this is "metadata" or "data about the data." As I began doing this with the data from Broadcom's new shipping system, I discovered that every customer in the new system had the wrong address associated with it.

When I shared this news with the Customer Service manager—that every shipment was about to go to the wrong place the next morning—she almost fainted and quickly got it fixed. Although she had logged into the new system, this wasn't obvious to her. It was only clear because I compared the entire data set to the old system. That could have been very bad not only for the company but also for her own career.

I share this story to illustrate how the data team is the face of IT for most business functions. Decision makers interact almost exclusively with the data that gets presented to them, however, that happens. The people who depend on information from the systems usually work with the data team. They are the first responders.

Tip of the IT Iceberg

Do you know anyone who can trace the path of that text message you sent from your phone today to your family in Florida? Seven layers, called the "OSI Model," make up the basic structure of internet communications: physical (like disks and wires), datalink (MAC addresses), network (IP addresses), transport (packets), session (communication channels), presentation (like character sets), and application (like http [web] or SMTP [email]).

The way network engineers remember this is by the mnemonic "Please Do Not Throw Sausage Pizza Away." Google this phrase, it's a great Jeopardy question.

It's like that with data management. People who work on a data team need a broad awareness of how things work, top to bottom. Here are some examples of how a centralized data team develops this end-to-end knowledge:

- When they see an automotive customer buying missile parts, they recognize the bad data because they understand customer end markets, not just the reporting technologies.
- They understand the business sensitivity of the data they're publishing, so they learn how to test end point security (like phones and laptops) to ensure confidential data isn't compromised.
- They explain to an accountant why their journal entry causes a balance mismatch to the sales ledger and then explain to network engineers why encryption protocols slow down database queries.
- Understanding the value of early visibility, they proactively link master data before an acquisition closes.
- They understand how different types of storage media affect database query performance.
- They speak in business terms, and the CFO feels confident asking them about a metric definition.

Reporting is just the tip of the iceberg, and the data team must influence the entire iceberg. This focused, high-scale team becomes domain architects, not rule followers. They influence business teams to *use* the systems as they should, and they influence IT teams to *change* the system where they should.

Here's an example. The sales team scoped out some very sophisticated logic to categorize their sales leads data into seven buckets. My team responded to this by profiling the data, causing them to notice that 99 percent of the data fell into three categories. This was a clue that led them to ask a lot of questions. They discovered that the other four categories were actually errors that the business teams could fix. Instead of adding logic to the system, the data team proposed an exception report that the business team could use to fix the bad data. This was a simple approach that reduced the amount of code, cleansed the whole data set, and simplified business decisions.

A good data team knows how to transform business requests into healthy data decisions that make business decisions clearer. "No" sounds less like "no" when they redirect people toward simpler solutions. But if the data team always says "yes" to every request, they probably have work to do in this area. That's the hidden value of a good data team: They improve the whole system landscape, not just the data platform.

Explaining the Value

As a leader of the data team, it's your job to explain that value to the rest of the company. You should explain it in both *cost* and *value.*

First, the cost. Centralizing the data team brings into focus not only the strategy but how those resources impact the work of every other team. The cost might look like a large number, but if you see your data team only as a cost center, you've missed the point. A centralized data team makes everyone else more efficient by allowing more time for decisions, using better data.

Then, value. How much are those "better decisions" worth? Here's a formula: The number of analysts in your company (a) times the number of decisions per quarter (d) times the average value of each decision (v) equals the total value (T) of your data strategy ($T = a \times d \times v$). Unlike most IT groups, a data team is best measured by business value rather than risk avoidance.

It's a "soft" number, obviously. People across the business will feel the value and recognize your team. You, the team manager, must go a step further: quantify it, advocate for it, promote it, and give credit where credit is due.

Part 2: Leading a Data Team

The Apple TV series "Severance," starring Adam Scott, does a terrific job exposing the dehumanizing nature of American corporate life in the 21st century. The main character, Mark S., leads a team of data workers "whose memories have been surgically divided between their work and personal lives; when a mysterious colleague appears outside of work, it begins a journey to discover the truth about their jobs." The show exposes the false idea that you can (or should) completely separate who you are at work from who you are outside of it.

Like Mark S., I subconsciously began to wonder if I had been lied to the whole time I'd worked in the corporate data world. Maybe the company line about teamwork was just a way to make everyone work harder and longer, as if what's good for the company and your boss is good for you. When I came to Maxim, I decided that if I really believed data could unify (or dis-unify) a company, my approach would need to change. Managing my own team would be the foundation for that unity, serving my team instead of using them.

Data should unify teams. If leading a data team is just another career accomplishment, you've missed the most rewarding part of the work: developing a trusted team. Here are three ways to foster a strong data team, where their work is transformative and their sum is greater than the parts.

First, be a listener. A data worker messaged me: "I had to witness a very cringy ritual today. A manager asks how we can prevent having bugs in code, and the employee answers that we need to do more thorough testing. And both pretend those words are not empty shells devoid of all meaning."

Sometimes managers become so goal-oriented that even their attempts at collaboration sound like detached demands to work harder and faster. People can tell when you're really listening and when you're not.

The people who work under your leadership have the clearest view of what motivates you. They can tell if you make decisions in your own best interest or theirs; kindness only goes so far if everyone knows you're only being nice as a means of getting people to accomplish your own goals. But your team trusts you more when you become a "servant leader" and put others above yourself. You've got to model this from the top; individual agendas don't play well in this space, and teamwork is critical.

The best way to convince people you care about them is to care about them. Do this by listening to their ideas. They care as much as you care, and when people see you've got enough humility to not always think you're the smartest person in the room, trust grows.

Second, create interdependency. Building a house involves many different trades: Framers, electricians, and plumbers must work together to complete the house. Similarly, data team members develop ownership of subdomains within the architecture. Someone may become the domain expert in master data, while another team member develops leadership in the visualization space.

Dividing up responsibilities by technical domains forces people on your team to depend on each other more. Most data projects touch all the different domains, so managing this way gets everyone involved in every project. It's easy for a manager to only care about getting a project done fast and to get this done by using the most talented team member to do everything. But interdependency really does improve quality and sustainability; it also makes the work more enjoyable.

Finally, measure impact. When cell phone makers figured out that adding a camera to a phone was a cool feature, people suddenly found new identities as photographers. People take billions of photos now, but it's done more to grow the amount of data storage in the world than the number of great photos. How many of those photos do you go back and look at?

Huge libraries of reports resulted from the easy-to-use report writing tools available today. But just making something easy (like writing reports or taking pictures) doesn't make the overall situation better.

Measuring report usage right from the beginning counteracts this problem.

Using *metadata* ("data about the data") proactively gives your data team constant visibility to system usage results. It encourages healthy decisions about project value and where to spend resources. For example, when everyone knows that you are tracking and publishing the data usage, they recognize the importance of listening to user requests while, at the same time, creating awareness of the danger of overbuilding solutions. Creating "analytics on the analytics" helps your whole team focus on solutioning together with the users: They focus on improving the data and reports users value the most instead of reacting to the loudest requestor.

Measure usage two ways: the number of people using the system and the intensity in which they use it. "Usage intensity" means how many times per user, per day people access the analytic system. If people use the system to its fullest potential, they will query data directly in the system at a rate as fast as they can think.* When you see hundreds of people accessing the system dozens or even hundreds of times each day, you know you've impacted the way they work. Instead of taking data offline and doing their own thing, they've started to trust the system. You've accelerated corporate decisions.

Connecting Vision to the Work

I argued at the beginning of this chapter that connecting people's work to a business vision best motivates a data team. Ken Venner, then CIO of Broadcom and one of my early mentors, has an amazing ability to connect everyone's job to a huge vision.

Ken always said, "IT should be like air: It should just be there. Your life depends on it, but you shouldn't have to think about it."

For my data team at Maxim, connecting the work to the vision started with a conference room and dry-erase markers. I call this "collaborative whiteboarding." The visuals you see in this book took shape

---

* Queries from a database that take longer than 2.5 seconds cause people to wait for the system.

on that whiteboard. We discussed and debated what the end state should look like, every week, together, communicating to my team that everyone participates in the design. Data teams make hundreds of changes to the system every quarter, and all of them impact business outcomes, big and small. Everyone on the team gets to know the "why" behind each decision.

We went through a lot of marker colors, drawing out table names and fields, data flows to and from databases, or mapping out business logic. It was clear to my new team that I had a design agenda, very specific ideas about what each of those should look like. But it was the collaboration that connected the dots between technical decisions and business outcomes. Investing time like this, thinking through solutions together, and relating technical decisions to business outcomes are a great way to develop team unity.

"We are on a mission," I told the team, "A mission to change the way this company thinks. Every design decision we make here today affects that."

That's the same mission I hope I've inspired you to pursue through this book. It's an enormously bold goal to improve decisions that a company makes. But I hope this book will help you, your team, and your entire company realize this goal—Frictionless Data—as you pursue becoming data-driven.

ACKNOWLEDGMENTS

A few individuals I met in the corporate world changed the entire trajectory of my personal experience along with my career. You've heard about some of them in this book: Bruce Kiddoo, who believed in me and challenged me more than anyone; Serge Feduleyev, who stretched my thought powers to places I never thought possible; Kimi Karasawa, who figured out how to connect my theoretical dots to reality at Broadcom; Ray Vincent, the OG of data drivenness; and Dave Bourgeois, who challenged me to think about the theory, not just the practice. Nothing you have read in this book would exist if any of these people had not entered my universe.

Most everything I've learned was gleaned from those I've worked with as a team: Santhosh Pandiri, Kevin Kurumada, Truman Scarborough, Pete Shaheen, Yakov Shkolnikov, JF Maitrot, Anne Chiang, Ammi Blankrot, Brian Tran, Chris Mitsch, Jason Freitas, Tracy Jones, and Walter Curd, to name a few. Every idea is better because of their work and feedback, and many of these ideas originate with them.

Then, the people who partnered with me, who brainstormed, mentored me, and built genuine friendships together through the work: John Weidman, Shawn Greene, Ryan Hill, Mark Cummins, Barry Hoban, Ken Venner, Dave Bourgeois, Steve Vermillion, Gaja Nagarajan, Jyothi Gorti, Geryl Winterowd, Babu Jadam, John Frazier, Cara Bilinski, Bimal Tripathi, Don McIntosh, Pritam Bhatt, Jennie Doyle, Dave Barton, Vickie Jette, Martha Ryan, Prasanthi Tummala, Candice Levert, Bernard Smet, Peter Glassey, Raj Saran, Kevin Kraus, and Jen Betz.

Finally, those closest to me through the writing process: Eric Cummings and Michael Cummings, who transformed my writing into a real book, and Mike Koelsch, who uplevels everything I do with real art. I'm still in awe of the expert skills of these guys and amazed that they applied them to my little project. This book doesn't happen without them.

And then Kellie, my true partner, who encouraged me to "go write" while I pursued this totally abstract idea. She thinks data nerds are cool.

Working with all of you made my experience one of the most dynamic experiences I could hope for. Hopefully, this book is a small way to give back. Thanks!

APPENDIX

Benchmarking

Everybody wants to rule the world.

—Tears For Fears, 1985

When Michael Scott asked Dwight Schrute, "What was the most inspiring advice I've ever given you?" Dwight replied, "Don't be an idiot."

Later, he explained: "Whenever I'm about to do something, I think, 'Would an idiot do that?' and if they would, I do not do that thing."

Dwight understood that, when it comes to making decisions, you need a good benchmark. And his rather low benchmark was not being an idiot. You've got to start somewhere.

I call this set of benchmarks the "Data Drivenness Index": seven characteristics of a decision process supported by data, key success factors I've learned from my last 25 years leading data teams. You'll have a hard time improving your data strategy if you can't measure progress, so use these categories to make a quick assessment of your current circumstances and help you understand where to begin your journey.

Defining the Index

I'll share some examples here for each characteristic and a few questions to help you assess your own capabilities. Many of the questions in my scoring system are presented as a "yes" or "no" choice, but it's rare that a company will be entirely one of the other, so score yourself on a sliding scale. To help you find where to start and identify specific projects to make improvements, I'll define each measure, share an example, and then give you a set of questions to think about.

Collaboration

Data collaboration describes how well people, departments, and levels of management work together to arrive at decisions using the data. Looking at the way teams interact with the data provides a concrete measure of overall collaboration.

How well do people and teams in your company work together, using the data as a measure? Here are some questions you can ask to grade your company.

> *Do multiple groups report metrics from the same source data?* If the data from your business systems gets exported to multiple teams for reporting, that means you probably have multiple versions of the same metric, but they're not systematically aligned, and different managers apply their own definitions without aligning across teams.
>
> *Do the data labels on your reports look more like business terms or system terms?* If a new person can't understand the reports or if different departments use different names for the same data, then the teams probably don't speak the same language.

Integration

Integration describes the way systems work together as a single unit. Data integration describes the extent to which the reporting systems present the data as a unified, single view of the truth.

An integrated data environment starts with an overall vision of how the systems work together. Without this, every business problem looks like an opportunity for programmers to create more code. Business partnering, on the other hand, looks for the best solution using *both* business process changes and IT data expertise.

Here are some questions you can ask to grade your company on integration.

Does your company have a single, consolidated view of its key decision data sets? For example, a single view of customer data, from lead to cash, gives decision makers an end-to-end data view of their business process. Does this data flow easily from the business systems to the reporting systems, or is the flow held together with glue and duct tape?

Do key reports match financial data automatically? For example, do the sales reports match the financial reports? Integrating data sets that are not part of the same business workflow opens communication between different parts of your company.

Does core master data look the same across all your systems? Business processes always share master data (like products or customers), even if the systems don't make it easier. How well you've synchronized this master data across the three core parts of the enterprise architecture (business, systems, and data) gives a clear measure of integration.

Does a change in a core driver (like a product price) immediately reflect in the consolidated financial forecast? Good data integration aligns systems not just with business processes but also with planning processes. A company that integrates both ranks high on the integration scale. The most advanced data strategies turn forecasting into "scenario modeling," meaning that the company can modify an input (like the price of a material) and see the impact on overall future results. If I'm describing something you've never seen before, then give your company a zero score on this capability.

Visibility

Visibility describes the extent to which your data helps people make decisions about the future. In other words, it measures the amount of "forward-looking" data in your system.

Big companies often dedicate large finance teams to make their best guesses about the future instead of sourcing consolidated, bottom-up planning data from the teams who really run the business. The more people your data solution includes in forecasting processes, the more visibility your company gets.

How well does your company use data to understand what's coming next? Are you able to recognize changes in business conditions as they happen? Here are some questions you can ask to help grade your company.

> *Does the reporting system automatically keep snapshots of previous data points?* If point-in-time snapshots are a standard feature for all data sets, your solution scores high on visibility because the system helps analysts quickly recognize changes. But if people normally keep their own data snapshots for future reference, your solution isn't helping them.
>
> *Do system generated reports include both "actual" and "plan" data? Do business managers see forecast data for their area?* Simply giving access to forward-looking data goes a long way to aligning the decisions of a company. Plan data is sensitive information, so the ability of your system to deliver just the data people need for their job gives a good indication of how it ranks on this benchmark.

Velocity

Velocity measures how quickly data travels through your systems *and* through your people. Your data structures either accelerate decision data or create bottlenecks.

Here are two questions you can ask to help benchmark your data solution.

> *Do top decision makers receive metric updates from the system or from people?* A high-velocity data solution delivers fully qualified data to decision makers, every day, all at the same time.
>
> *How long does it take for an organization change to get reflected in all reports?* Organizational changes are one of the most common challenges of a data solution. It's the true test of data agility. A high-velocity data solution updates every report available to users the same day that the organization structure change gets made.

Reliability

Reliability measures how well a data solution handles unexpected technical events (like a data transfer interruption) and unexpected changes to the data (like an invalid price or customer). This includes good controls for error handling.

A good system should become more resilient over time, not just because it has great controls and architecture but also because the people managing it care enough to take corrective action on every unexpected issue. Analytic systems live at the end of the data food chain; they require the most robust awareness of error handling methods.

Here are some questions you can use to benchmark your solution.

> *When the numbers or other data are wrong, who notices first, the IT department or the users?* A good data strategy proactively recognizes issues with the data before it becomes available for use.

This could be visual controls and reviews of key reports, or systematic checkpoints in the data processing.

Do key metrics get delivered hands-free, even on weekends? A good data solution doesn't require anyone to handhold the processing. When IT teams and users fully trust its reliability, they allow the system itself to distribute reports to executives, even on weekends with the office lights off.

Value

Measuring value includes comparing the portfolio of reports and data solutions to both utilization and cost. A good data strategy requires investment, but just spending money isn't the best indicator of success.

The second most frustrating situation for an IT team is when they work tirelessly delivering data only to hear executives, say, they don't have the data they need for decisions. The first most frustrating situation, however, is working hard to build a solution only to find out that nobody ever uses it. Companies often see value as lowering the overhead cost of the system, but a good data strategy measures it by how much value users get from the data.

Do people outside the IT department work in data management? "Shadow IT" describes the cost to a company when teams outside the IT department fill in data gaps with their own solutions. It's a hidden cost both in the amount spent and the missed opportunities for aligned decisions.

Do you know the number of reports your company publishes? A good data team measures this and aligns their work with the value business teams assign to solutions based on the report usage.

Accessibility

Accessibility measures the complexity of the normal path *people* take to get to the data. It also measures the ease of use once they access the data.

Do analysts regularly spend time exporting data to spreadsheets? A good data strategy helps people use the system for decisions instead of forcing them to take data out of the system.

Do you limit data users to a single access role? When people struggle to find the data they need, their default reaction is to ask for more access. A good data strategy assigns permissions that give people exactly what they need to do their job with a single access profile and nothing more.

Is it difficult for a user to get matching detailed data for a key metric? A good data strategy makes it easy to navigate from a metric to the business transaction or forecast behind the metric. When people need to navigate to a different system or a different report to see the details behind a metric, it's not easily accessible.

NOTES

Preface

1. Keller, 110.
2. Keller, *Every Good Endeavor*, 111.

How to Read This Book

1. Kissinger, Schmidt and Huttenlocher, *ChatGPT Heralds an Intellectual Revolution—WSJ*.

Chapter 1

1. Sweet, "Emphasis Is Mine," *CNBC*.

Chapter 3

1. Ross, Weill, and Robertson, *Enterprise Architecture as Strategy*.
2. Arena, *Adaptive Space*.

Chapter 4

1. Newport, *A World Without Email*, 141.
2. Ibid, 142.

Chapter 10

1. Ross, Weill, and Robertson, *Enterprise Architecture as Strategy*, 94.

REFERENCES

Arena, M. 2018. *Adaptive Space*, New York,NY: McGraw-Hill.

Cal Newport. *A World Without Email*, 142

Cal Newport. 2021. *A World Without Email*, 141. New York, NY, Portfolio.142.

Carr, N. 2025. *Superbloom: How Technologies of Connection Tear Us Apart*, W.W. Norton & Company.

Julie Sweet. 2023. *Interview by CNBC*, June 22, 2023.

Keller, T. 2012. *Every Good Endeavor*, 110. New York, NY: Penguin Books.

Ibid, 111.

Ross, J.W., P. Weill, and D.C. Robertson. 2006. *Enterprise Architecture as Strategy*, 94. Harvard Business Review Press.

BIBLIOGRAPHY

Augustine, and R.S. Pine-Coffin. *Confessions*. Penguin Books, 2003.

Ganesan, K. *The Business Case for AI: A Leader's Guide to AI Strategies, Best Practices & Real-World Applications*. Opinosis Analytics Publishing, 2022.

Gladwell, M. *The Tipping Point*. Abacus, 2013.

Keller, T., and K.L. Alsdorf. *Every Good Endeavor: Connecting Your Work to God's Work*. Penguin Books, an Imprint of Penguin Random House, 2016.

Lewis, M. *Moneyball*. WW Norton, 2004.

Marr, B. *Data Strategy: How to Profit From a World of Big Data, Analytics and Artificial Intelligence*. Kogan Page, 2022.

Newport, C. *A World Without Email: Reimagining Work in an Age of Communication Overload*. Portfolio/Penguin, an Imprint of Penguin Random House LLC, 2021.

Thaler, R.H., and C.R. Sunstein. *Nudge: The Final Edition*. Penguin Books, 2022.

ABOUT THE AUTHOR

Zane Hall led data teams at some of the biggest semiconductor companies in the world: Texas Instruments, Broadcom Corporation, Maxim Integrated, and Analog Devices. In 2023, he started consulting and writing his first book to help as many companies as possible improve their data strategies. He serves on the board of Common Ground Surf, a mentoring movement for underserved children in Huntington Beach, California.

Hall publishes a weekly newsletter to help people with practical, counterintuitive ideas that remove friction from their decision data (www.zanehall.substack.com). He also serves as board chairman of Common Ground Surf (www.thecommongorund.org), a mentoring movement for underserved children in Huntington Beach, California.

INDEX

.

www.ingramcontent.com/pod-product-compliance
Lightning Source LLC
Chambersburg PA
CBHW061218220326
41599CB00025B/4684